Henri Nouwen &

The Return of the Prodigal Son

GABRIELLE EARNSHAW

*The Making of
a Spiritual Classic*

PARACLETE PRESS
Brewster, Massachusetts

2020 First Printing

Henri Nouwen and The Return of the Prodigal Son:
The Making of a Spiritual Classic

Copyright © 2020 by Gabrielle Earnshaw

ISBN 978-1-64060-169-7

The Paraclete Press name and logo (dove on cross) are trademarks of Paraclete Press, Inc.

Library of Congress Cataloging-in-Publication Data
Names: Earnshaw, Gabrielle, author.
Title: Henri Nouwen and the Return of the prodigal son : the making of a
  spiritual classic / Gabrielle Earnshaw.
Description: Brewster, Massachusetts : Paraclete Press, 2020. | Includes
  bibliographical references and index. | Summary: "Earnshaw provides a
  detailed account of how the book came to be written, shedding light on
  Nouwen's writing process and aspects of his life experience that
  influenced his insights and ideas"-- Provided by publisher.
Identifiers: LCCN 2019053060 | ISBN 9781640601697 (trade paperback)
Subjects: LCSH: Nouwen, Henri J. M. | Catholic Church--Clergy--Biography. |
  Nouwen, Henri J. M. Return of the prodigal son. | Spiritual
  life--Catholic Church. | Rembrandt Harmenszoon van Rijn, 1606-1669.
  Return of the prodigal son.
Classification: LCC BX4705.N87 E37 2020 | DDC 248.4/82--dc23

10 9 8 7 6 5 4 3 2 1

Published by Paraclete Press
Brewster, Massachusetts
www.paracletepress.com
Printed in the United States of America

Contents

Introduction

The same year Henri Nouwen published his masterwork *The Return of the Prodigal Son* he turned sixty years old. To celebrate this milestone birthday, the L'Arche Daybreak community, where Nouwen had lived for the previous six years, planned a special party for him. As part of the festivities, Robert Morgan, a friend of Daybreak and a professional clown, asked Nouwen to dress up in blue balloon pants with a matching shirt and a ruffled burgundy-colored collar. Robert placed a beanie on Nouwen's head and had him crawl into a large sack that was dragged to the middle of a large room. Giggles erupted from the gathered audience of his Daybreak friends. Then, with some instruction from Robert, Nouwen began to emerge from the pulsating sack. At first, all you could see was a skinny, bare foot poking out. Then, with his natural flair for the dramatic, Nouwen started making little chirping sounds as he stuck out more limbs. Finally, Nouwen sprang out, leapt to his feet, raised his enormous hands in the air, and gave the audience the wide-eyed, delighted look of a child. His rebirth as a clown was complete.

A video recording of this birthday drama is preserved in the Nouwen Archives at the University of St. Michael's College, Toronto. It reveals how natural this shift from adult man to baby clown was for Nouwen. His sense of play was matched only by his capacity for understanding the symbolism he enacted. Later that evening, speaking to Daybreak friends about the party, he expressed his deep gratitude to them: "You know me. You really know me." And they did. After years of searching, Nouwen had found his home.

The clown birthday is a vivid metaphor for a spiritual rebirth that began for Nouwen in the fall of 1983 when, exhausted and adrift, he first saw the poster that would change his life: *The Return of the Prodigal Son* by Rembrandt Harmenszoon van Rijn.

At the time, Nouwen was living at La Ferme in the village of Trosly-Breuil, France, spending a few months at L'Arche, a community that offers a home to people with intellectual disabilities. He was there to recuperate from an extensive US speaking tour he had just completed before he moved to Cambridge, Massachusetts, where he would join the faculty at Harvard Divinity School for the 1984 fall semester. One day, he went to visit his friend Simone Landrien in the community's small documentation center and saw the Rembrandt poster pinned to her door. All Nouwen saw at this moment was a boy being embraced by a gentle father. As he shares so vividly in his book, a flood of emotion overwhelmed him and awakened a yearning for love and safety that would shape the course of his life for years to come.

This encounter with the Rembrandt poster marks the genesis of his spiritual classic *The Return of the Prodigal Son: A Story of a Homecoming*, a book that reached "term" nine years later after a series of life-altering experiences. Nouwen would leave Harvard, suffer a nervous breakdown, survive a life-threatening accident, reconcile important relationships, and perhaps most importantly, join the L'Arche Daybreak community in Toronto as pastor. Nouwen had to live the painting before he could write about it.

The Return of the Prodigal Son captures Nouwen's wisdom on the questions that animate many of us: Who is God? Who am I? How should I live? He writes on identity, God, relationships, and above all, the unifying, undergirding nature of love itself. It is the book that most fully expresses his long journey to freedom.

What is this freedom? According to Nouwen, it is to enter a second childhood as expressed by Jesus, who said, "Truly I tell you, unless you change and become like little children, you will never enter the kingdom of heaven" (Matthew 18:3). It is a movement away from compulsions and addictions to a life of spiritual maturity, one in which we forgive others, serve them, and form a new bond of fellowship with them.

To enter a second childhood while claiming a new adulthood is to live a paradox. We can allow ourselves to be more childlike (in contrast with childish) in our approach to life. We can live our mature years with renewed wonder and awe. We can shed aspects of ourselves that we no longer need, and unify the essentials left over once the stripping is done. Entering a second childhood is to integrate all that we have experienced into a whole—and enter life as though born again.

In *The Return of the Prodigal Son,* Nouwen lets go of the compulsion to run away from difficulties, to hold on to fear, to cling to resentment and childish fantasies. By letting them all go he comes home to himself. Gradually, he steps into an entirely new way of being. He becomes as the Father in the painting, a blessing and vessel of love to the world.

This is not to say that Nouwen's journey was easy. As readers, we are awed at the way he shares his vulnerability and neediness along the way. Yet, we sense Nouwen's strength and resolve to persevere in his search—not for an outward prize, but for the reward of allowing himself to be loved by God. At the end of the book, Nouwen is not perfect, nor is the journey over, but he has been changed.

Nouwen shows us that we too can return home. We have not ruined everything with our bad choices, doubts, or shortcomings. We can start again. We can be reborn. And our loving God will run to meet us.

The book speaks to the many people who feel unworthy of being received back by God after turning away. One critic suggests that *The Return of the Prodigal Son* is a book "for sinners," in that it resonates with people who feel that they have failed God in some way and are unworthy of God's attention and love. Nouwen offers a new image of God that many of his generation wouldn't recognize—a God who is merciful and unconditionally loving. A God who uses power not to control or dominate but to restore, console, and bless.

Nouwen's road to the insights he had about the parable was a long one. This book is about how he got to the point where he could say, "I will be the father even while I know it will be a most dreadful emptiness." This is a surprising conclusion to draw from the parable. Where did this insight about spiritual maturity come from? Where did he get the strength for this courageous choice? What happened in the years between seeing the poster for the first time when he yearned to be enfolded in the arms of the loving father—to the realization that he was being called to be the father? Between yearning to be blessed to being the one who blesses? What happened in his life to allow such profound insights into the heart of the son, the elder brother, and finally the near-blind father?

In the first chapter, I explore what led to the moment of Nouwen's collapse in front of the poster. What primed him to be so ready to see the poster as "his painting"? I explore his earliest relationships with his family in the Netherlands and how as a sensitive child, patriarchal norms of fatherhood and hands-off mothering philosophies of the time created perfect conditions for neediness and anxiety in Nouwen. We will see that this led to patterns of trying to please others in order to get the sense of safety and love that he craved. Nouwen was lonely when he saw the poster for the first time. He needed the love of a gentle father. He was also grappling with his sexuality as he lived his vow of celibacy. As you will see,

Rembrandt's painting was a doorway to reconcile these fragments of discontent and unease.

Chapter 2 is about Nouwen's intellectual formation and how it informed *The Return of the Prodigal Son*. What people, methods, and theories influenced how he wrote about the painting? I look at how Nouwen used visual art as a means of understanding his life and the world. Art fed his spiritual vision long before he saw the poster. We will see that *visio divina*, an ancient contemplative practice of encountering the divine through images, informed his reaction to the painting and gave him the ability to see it with the eyes of his heart. He could enter into the Rembrandt painting so fruitfully because he had been cultivating a spiritual vision for decades before he saw it. Next, I explore the foundational importance of Anton Boisen to Nouwen's life and thought. Boisen is considered by many to be the father of pastoral theology. It was Boisen who introduced Nouwen to the concept of studying people as "living human documents." This approach of listening to, analyzing, and understanding people's life stories fed into all of Nouwen's later work. One cannot understand Henri Nouwen or his interpretation of Rembrandt's painting without examining the work of Boisen.

The third chapter addresses Nouwen's writing process. What went into writing the book? How many drafts did it take? Who helped him? What was happening in his life in the nine years that it took to complete it? This chapter is informed by a careful analysis of early drafts of the book as well as an examination of the letters exchanged between Nouwen and his publisher at Doubleday and other important parties. With these archival sources, we are able to get inside the process as it was unfolding, particularly the primary importance of his friend Sue Mosteller, a sister of the Congregation of St. Joseph and member of L'Arche Daybreak, who pushed Nouwen to claim his identity as the father. We see through an intimate exchange of letters between

Mosteller and Nouwen, all of which are being published here for the first time, how central she was to the writing of the book. This chapter also explores the historical context of the book's publication. Whereas the first part of the chapter zooms in on the progress of the book from genesis to publication, this section zooms out to place *The Return of the Prodigal Son* in its broader social and cultural context. What other books on similar themes came out around this time? How did Nouwen's book compare? In what ways was he speaking to the *zeitgeist*? I notice that in 1992 the "boomer" generation was longing for new ways to express and feed their spiritual impulses. I show that Nouwen spoke to this generational need and gave them a revised image of the Divine that spoke to their desire for a God of compassion. I show how he gave them (and us) a new entryway into the beauty and scope of Jesus's message of love. You will see that while Nouwen's very Christian and Jesus-centered book precluded acclaim by popular culture, it shared many characteristics of the self-help and "spiritual but not religious" works of the time, particularly those that, like *The Return of the Prodigal Son*, drew on psychology, parables, and archetypes to speak to the needs of the day.

The fourth chapter focuses on the book's impact. How did critics respond? What did his readers have to say? We see that although the book did not receive much attention from the media, reader response was enthusiastic. I look at letters that Nouwen received from his readers and draw out some of the most common reactions. We hear from a prisoner in Ghana whose experience of solitary confinement was changed by his reading of the book, from mothers and fathers struggling with estrangement from their children on how the book gives them courage to wait in joy rather than anger or fear for their return, and we learn of the many people for whom the book changed their relationship with God, and also with themselves. The book opens doors for readers to claim their worthiness of love.

We also look at letters from a minority of readers who were more critical. "Why don't you look at the female figures in the painting?" wrote several women. "Your depiction of the prodigal son's return celebrates his 'being tamed.' Why does religion smother his youthful, spirited, passionate impulses?" asked one reader. This chapter concludes with a look at the book's more famous readers, as well as other indicators of how it has inspired contemporary artists to express their experience of the parable and the painting.

Chapter 5 covers Nouwen's life after the book was published. What impact did it have on Nouwen's life? Was his aspiration to claim fatherhood ultimately lived out? We see that indeed Nouwen's life was transformed by "his painting" and that while he never completely overcame his struggles, he was able to live them in a new way. We hear testimonials from people who lived with him after the book was written who describe his almost insatiable desire to welcome and bless members of his Daybreak community. He proclaimed the truth of their belovedness with deep conviction and even urgency. We see that his writing vocation accelerated; he wrote eleven books in four years. This chapter ends with a glimpse of a new "painting" that captured his imagination—a trapeze troupe. His imagination, having absorbed all he could from the Rembrandt image, was captivated by a new expression of God's reality in our lives.

The final chapter looks at where we are nearly a quarter century later. *The Return of the Prodigal Son* is Henri Nouwen's bestselling book. It has sold more than one million copies worldwide and has been translated into thirty-four languages. It continues to outsell all his other books. What accounts for the book's lasting influence? In what ways is it dated? Prescient? Is it relevant for today's seekers? I begin by considering Nouwen as prophet, in the sense that he holds up a mirror to ourselves and also to the societal norms of our day. He helps us see our infatuation with youthfulness, our propensity for self-rejection, and how our norms of masculinity distort our image of God. I conclude with speculation rather than answers. I have noted that in subtle ways, *The Return of the Prodigal Son* indicates that Nouwen seems to have been heading into a territory beyond religious literalism and a gendered/binary God—a direction that many today will welcome and others will find challenging. But this is only my opinion, and as readers of *The Return of the Prodigal Son* will appreciate, you may disagree. But this is not a problem. This is an invitation to strike your own path toward a life filled with love, hope, and meaning.

A Note About Sources

I have used a variety of sources to piece together the story of how Henri Nouwen's book *The Return of the Prodigal Son* came into being. The majority of sources are unpublished and are housed in The Henri J. M. Nouwen Archives and Research Collection at the University of St. Michael's College, University of Toronto. As the founding archivist for the Nouwen Archives, a position I held for sixteen years, and now as the chief archivist for the Henri Nouwen Legacy Trust, I have a deep knowledge of what material is available for research.

Fortunately, Henri Nouwen kept meticulous records of his writing process. He created files for each book he wrote and this one is no different. The *Prodigal Son* files I had access to consist of draft manuscripts, notes and comments from his "first" readers for each draft, notes, and revisions from his paid copyeditor Conrad Wieczorek, as well as the totality of his correspondence with his publisher, Doubleday. Information about the Dutch and German editions (which were issued ahead of the American edition) was also readily available in Nouwen's correspondence files.

In addition to the early drafts of the manuscripts kept by Henri Nouwen himself, I relied on two other sources to trace the chronology of his writing process. One is a typed manuscript that was donated to the Nouwen Archives in 2010. This is what I consider to be the earliest draft of the book. It was written in 1987 and is referred to as the Turner accession (based on the name of the donor). The second is a recording of a retreat that Henri Nouwen gave on the prodigal son in June 1988. This retreat was given in Quebec, Canada, to L'Arche assistants and is referred to as the "Returning" retreat. The transcript from this retreat was eventually edited as *Home Tonight* by Sue Mosteller (Doubleday, 2009). At times I quote from the transcript of the retreat and others times from Mosteller's edited work.

In addition to these sources, I relied on correspondence between Nouwen and his close friends Sue Mosteller, Nathan Ball, and others; readers' letters to Henri Nouwen; administrative files regarding his work as pastor for L'Arche Daybreak; oral history interviews from the Henri Nouwen Oral History Project; Nouwen's collected material on Anton Boisen that I refer to in chapter 2; and drafts of an unfinished work about the spirituality of the trapeze, known as the Circus Book. Finally, at times I rely on conversations I have had with key figures in Henri Nouwen's life, including his brother Laurent Nouwen, Sue Mosteller, and Peter Naus.

All quotations of Henri Nouwen from published works will be noted in the text using abbreviations. Quotations from unpublished archival sources and other authors will include a footnote to the source.

A bibliography of all works cited (published and unpublished) is available at the end of the book.

All archival sources have been gratefully published with permission of the Henri Nouwen Legacy Trust.

Henri Nouwen &

The Return of the Prodigal Son

Chapter 1 ~◎
The Collapse, November 1983

*In the hero stories, the call to go on a journey takes the form of
a loss, an error, a wound, an unexplainable longing, or a sense
of a mission. When any of these happens to us, we are being
summoned to make a transition. It will always mean leaving
something behind. . . . The paradox here is that loss is a path
to gain.*

—David Richo[1]

Nouwen walked into Simone Landrien's office and saw the
Rembrandt poster for the first time. Feeling lost and exhausted, he
found the image of the father blessing his son touched a place inside
him that had "never been reached before" (*Prodigal Son*, 4). What
led to this moment of collapse in front of the prodigal son poster and
made Nouwen feel "like a vulnerable little child who wanted to crawl
onto its mother's lap and cry" (*Prodigal Son*, 4)? What made his heart
"leap" when he saw it (*Prodigal Son*, 4)?

From a very early age, Henri Nouwen was on a quest. What
he was searching for and how he went about finding it varied and
took many forms as he grew up. But, fundamentally, Nouwen was
searching for intimacy. He searched for bonds of love that would
satisfy his need for safety and belonging.

By all accounts, Nouwen came from a loving, stable family, but
in his words, "Somehow fear of being rejected, of being abandoned,

of being disliked has been with me as long as I can remember. I kept asking my parents, friends and colleagues in many different ways: 'Do you love me?' And I never heard a clear Yes that I could receive. I kept doubting, wondering, searching and begging for a final clear and total Yes, but it never seemed to come."[2]

"Do you love me?" was his primal cry for love and affection. It was a reaching-out for affirmation that perplexed his parents, Maria and Laurent. This yearning for love, what he calls "special love" (*Home Tonight*, xvii), is one of Nouwen's signature character traits. Many of his life decisions make sense in view of this dominant feature of his personality.

The search for love imbued Nouwen with curiosity and a sense of adventure as well as restlessness and dissatisfaction. It led him to join the priesthood and to a lifelong love affair with God. It also led to dark nights of the soul when loneliness and depression overwhelmed him.

His first book, *Intimacy*, published in 1969 when he was thirty-seven years old, explored this foundational quest. In *Intimacy*, the search for love is equated with the search for home. In the Introduction, Nouwen says he will address "the seldom articulated and often unrecognized desire for a real home in this world" (*Intimacy*, 2).

The word *home* conjures up images of safety, rest, and familial bonds. Home, if we are fortunate, is often a place of unity, integration, and freedom. These are the objects of Nouwen's quest—as a baby in the crib reaching out for his parents, in 1969 as a young scholar writing his first book, in 1983 when he sees the Rembrandt poster for the first time. Nouwen is on a quest for home. The painting hits him "like a bolt of lightning" (as he describes it in an early draft of the manuscript—the Turner accession) because here, in the magical light of Rembrandt's painting, he finally catches a glimpse of it.

The Return of the Prodigal Son has many characteristics of a spiritual-quest narrative. Like all hero or heroine stories, Nouwen begins with a classic opener: "One day I went to visit my friend . . ." He describes his state of mind: "I was exhausted from a self-exposing speaking tour." He creates an instant rapport with his listeners by sharing his vulnerability: "I was anxious, lonely, restless, and very needy." When describing the feeling of seeing the poster for the first time, he uses a biblical quote, "My heart leapt when I saw it," referencing the passage in Luke when Elizabeth hears Mary's greeting and her baby "leaped in her womb." As in Luke's Gospel, this detail foreshadows a spiritual event to come. It has a suggestive quality of larger mysteries to unfold. The pregnancy imagery hints at a rebirth.

He draws us deeper into his story by describing a series of trials—his breakdown after moving to L'Arche following the dissolution of an important relationship, the accident that left him close to death, reconciliation with his father that called him to a new vocation of blessing and forgiveness.

While Nouwen travels a far physical distance in his journey, the tale he tells in *The Return of the Prodigal Son* is ultimately an interior one. Like heroes or heroines in myths and fairy tales, Nouwen gains wisdom from his trials and is transformed. He moves from seeker to the one found. He has new ears to hear the answer to his lifelong search for love and it fills his soul—"You are my Son, the Beloved; with you I am well pleased" (Mark 1:11). Finally, like heroes or heroines before him, he goes on to share these "pearls of great price" with us, and with the story told we are left to ponder how we will navigate our own quest.

Search for The Father's Love

While Henri Nouwen's life can be viewed through the lens of a spiritual quest, another way to see it is as a search for a father's love—both human and divine.

In *The Return of the Prodigal Son*, Nouwen mentions his father, Laurent Nouwen Sr., three times. In two instances, the mention is in passing—one is about clothing that his parents bought him, and the second is about looking in the mirror and seeing his dad in his own image. In the third instance, however, Nouwen tells us a bit more about this central relationship in his life. He describes an incident from 1989, when after being critically injured in a road accident near his Daybreak home, he told his father, who had flown from Holland with his sister Laurien to be with him, something he had never shared with him before.

While recovering after surgery, he explicitly told his father that he loved him and was grateful to receive his love. He shared other thoughts and feelings he had never verbalized, and was surprised by how long it had taken him to do so. His father was puzzled by it all, but received his words with a smile. Nouwen experienced this encounter as a "spiritual event" that allowed him to "return from a false dependence on a human father who cannot give me all I need to a true dependence on the divine Father" (*Prodigal Son*, 78).

We sense that Nouwen forgives his father for not giving him everything he needed, or perhaps that Nouwen has reached a point where he realizes that what he needs is more than any human father could provide. It becomes a pivotal moment in Nouwen's life.

While this event is told in a few paragraphs in *The Return of the Prodigal Son*, in early attempts to write the book (which we will look at in more depth in later chapters), Nouwen is more explicit about his experience of his father and male authority figures in general. He writes, "I know the desire to be independent from a father who is strong, powerful and dominating. Whether I speak of my Dad, my bishop, the dean of the school or the leader of the community—there has always been the fearful father who knows things before you have told him, understands before you have explained, answers before you have asked and decides before you have voiced your opinion."[3]

While leading a retreat on the prodigal son in 1988 for members of L'Arche, Nouwen fleshed out his experience of his father further. There, he explained that he had always longed for his father's approval but never seemed to get it.

"You see," he explained to his retreatants, "my father accomplished his goals late in life by becoming a successful professor of law, and based on his background this rise to fame was quite unusual in his day. My dad was very bright and able to function well in the world of competition. I, as the older son in our family, seemed to be programmed to believe that I had to be at least as good as my dad. Thus began a lifelong competition with respect to our careers and to most other subjects as well" (*Home Tonight*, 69).

As Nouwen was aware, his experience of his father was unique to him. As the eldest of four children, he would have had a different relationship with his father than would his younger siblings. Peter Naus, a social psychologist who attended seminary with Nouwen and visited the family on occasion, remembers a difficult dynamic in the family in which Laurent Nouwen Sr. was competitive with Nouwen and the youngest daughter, Laurien, but not with sons Paul and Laurent. While basically a loving father, he often responded to Nouwen's ideas with "I could have told you that long ago!" (see *Home Tonight*, 69).

Naus observed that it was the role of the mother, Maria Nouwen, to soften the impact of the father. According to Naus, "She represented gentleness. . . . She brought warmth into the family. When she entered the room there was warmth."[4] Naus also remembers that while Laurent Nouwen Sr. presented an authoritative persona he could also be "mischievous" and "not so serious."

Laurent Nouwen Sr., like many men of his generation (and ours too), felt intense social pressure to make something of himself. He was successful, but he felt the need to keep working hard to maintain his status. He did what he had to do for his family, but he was not a man of emotions, not one to show his vulnerability. He projected power and strength. He valued the intellect and cerebral pursuits. It is likely he worried about his sensitive and needy son.

In a journal written in the year of his death, Nouwen would reflect on his family dynamic this way:

> It was my mother who offered closeness, affection, and personal care. My father seemed more distant. He was the provider who loved his wife, expected much of his children, worked hard, and discussed important issues. A virtuous, righteous man, but I found it difficult to feel intimate with him. (*Sabbatical Journey, 81–82*)

Laurent Nouwen Sr. may have seemed emotionally distant to Nouwen, but his actions spoke of his love for his son. He visited Nouwen regularly in the United States. He wrote and called frequently. He was always available—just not in the way that Nouwen longed for. Nouwen felt his father didn't affirm him. He didn't read his books. He didn't brag to his friends about his son's accomplishments the way he did about Nouwen's brother Paul, who was on the news most evenings speaking as the director of the Royal Dutch Touring Club, ANWB; or Nouwen's other brother Laurent, a lawyer and partner at the distinguished law firm Nauta Dutilh in Rotterdam.

"Work-to-Earn-Love" Ethos

While acknowledging the complexity of the relationship and its ultimate unknowability, what we might consider is that Nouwen experienced a father with a "work-to-earn-love" ethos. From his father he learned that worldly success was a means to gaining love (see *Home Tonight*, 69–70). As a student and later as a young adult, Nouwen worked very hard to meet this criteria for love. He acquired multiple academic degrees; he published scores of books and was honored with awards and prestigious faculty appointments.

In this light, it is understandable why Rembrandt's poster hit him so hard. He was exhausted from having to prove himself in order to earn love. Seeing Rembrandt's depiction of the father, Nouwen collided with his own unfulfilled longing. In an early draft of *The Return of the Prodigal Son* he gave words to this experience: "It was the gentle forgiving touch of two hands that remained with me, reminded me of a love that cannot be earned or gained, but which is there simply to be received in gratitude."[5]

In 1983, the many years of being a pleaser had finally caught up with him. At Harvard, he was lonely and alienated by academic competitiveness. Earlier, as a missionary in Peru (something he tried in the 1980s), his difficulty with the Spanish language precluded deep friendships and meaningful contact. A ten-city speaking tour on a very volatile subject—American complicity in oppressive regimes in Central and Latin America—had left him completely exhausted and burned out.[6] On top of all this, the "special love" of his mother had been stilled by her death in 1978.

In his "Returning" retreat, Nouwen reflected on the effect of her death on him:

Although I loved teaching in the universities I was always yearning for intimacy in my life. I found this special love to a certain degree in my relationship with my mother. She loved me in a particular way, followed my every move, faithfully corresponded with me, expressing a love that was so tangible, full and close to be being unconditional. When she died in 1978 during my time at Yale, I grieved her absence in a very profound place inside. . . . Her absence plunged me into a downward spiral so that my final teaching years at Harvard in the early 1980s were some of the unhappiest in my life. (*Home Tonight*, xvii)

Nouwen longed for more than his father could give him. He thirsted for affirmation, and at numerous points in his life he found surrogate father figures to meet this need. One example can be seen in a letter he wrote to his friend Richard, a political activist he met in Mexico in the early 1960s:

From the moment I met you in Cuernavaca I have felt a deep and strong attraction to you. It wasn't a sexual attraction as much as an attraction to your inner strength, your ability to give me affection and care, your interest in me and your opening to me a world of feeling and thought that were very new to me. Your embrace, your touch, your smile, your strong hands, they all gave me a feeling of safety and protection. I often felt in your presence as a child who is safe because daddy's close. Emotionally I often wanted to be loved by you as by a father.[7]

Years later, Nouwen was similarly drawn to John Eudes Bamberger, the abbot of the Trappist Abbey of the Genesee in upstate New York, with that similar intensity. His relationship with Jean Vanier can be seen as another example.[8] Eventually, Nouwen would finally meet the father figure he needed, but it would not come in the form that he was expecting.

Fathers and Sons

To understand Nouwen's longing for intimacy with a loving father in a more rounded way, we need to consider the context of the times in which he lived. What were the societal norms around displays of affection between fathers and sons? How did society regard men who showed their emotions or vulnerabilities? Patriarchy has historically dictated that men behave in a certain way. Society says, "Real men don't cry" and "Act like a man!"

Perhaps not much has changed. Even today we live in a society that longs for a father's loving touch, and we see very little of it around, particularly between fathers and sons. We are generations of children longing for a gentle father. What role models do we have today for fatherhood? Nouwen was asking similar questions in the early days of his academic career.

In 1970, Nouwen published an article called "Generation Without Fathers" in *Commonweal* magazine. He was teaching pastoral theology at the University of Notre Dame while holding a similar teaching position at a seminary in Utrecht, the Netherlands. The article is about Christian leadership in an era of unprecedented anti-authoritarianism in the West. Nouwen draws on psychological training he had taken after ordination to identify a new Western phenomenon—young people were no longer looking to traditional authority figures for help. They saw their parents as complicit in the atrocities of the world wars, powerless in the face of nuclear and environmental threats, and narrow in their worldviews. They were ready to abandon the Father completely and chart their own way in the world.[9]

Nouwen, one with this generation and also its observer, described it this way: "[There is] no desire anymore to leave the safe place and to travel to the father's house which has so many rooms, no hope to reach the promised land or to see Him who is waiting for his prodigal son, no ambition to sit at the right or the left side of the Heavenly Throne."[10]

Some two decades after he wrote this, Nouwen was still circling the question of how to reconcile with the Father, both personally and in the broader context of society. This time, twenty years older and now entering middle age, he focuses not on youthful rejection of the father but the moment we heed the call of homecoming and come face-to-face with the Father. In this sense, *The Return of the Prodigal Son* is the story of a generation reexamining its relationship to God and authority figures. Nouwen, using his own life as an example, shows that we can stop behaviors that keep us in perpetual distance from the Father. We can accept our sonship or daughtership without losing our freedom. And eventually, we can take our place not "at the right or the left side of the Heavenly Throne," but as Father/Mother ourselves.

Recently, two Catholic thinkers, Laurence Freeman of the World Community of Christian Meditation, and Richard Rohr, the popular Franciscan friar and priest, used social media to remind their followers that our propensity for conflating our images of father and God comes from long-held belief in a punitive God that must be appeased with sacrifice.

Freeman wrote,

Much more often, our image of God is related not to those experiences of love, of joy, or of union, but it's related to experiences of authority and punishment. A young child is taught to think of God as a sort of super parent. The very word we use about God, of course, Father, carries with it, in most children's upbringing, an image of a person in the family who does the correction, who does the discipline. The idea of God as Father carries with it, therefore, this sense of control, this sense of dominance. And where there is punishment or this kind of relationship to authority, there is usually fear. We fear being punished, we fear being sent to hell.[11]

Rohr put it this way:

In authoritarian and patriarchal cultures, most people were fully programmed to think this way—working to appease an authority figure who was angry, punitive, and even violent in "his" reactions. Many still operate this way, especially if they had an angry, demanding, or abusive parent. People respond to this kind of God, as sick as it is, because it fits their own story line.[12]

As both Rohr and Freeman say, it is deep within our collective and individual psyches to think of God as a punitive parent. *The Return of the Prodigal Son* is so powerful because Nouwen, without speaking a word of theology or history, addresses this metanarrative with a gentle story of his own. He invites people to listen to his own experience of releasing this shaming image and to embrace an image of a feminine/masculine creator who envelops us in unearned, unconditional love. Nouwen uses the power of story to help us revise our image of God so we can allow God's love to enter our lives with freedom and even joy.

Search for Intimacy

Nouwen sees the poster and has a visceral reaction. His body responds—his heart leaps in his chest. As much as he wants his father's approval and love, he longs for the father's touch. In an early draft of the book, he writes, "[The poster] seemed to respond to my own deepest yearnings, my own most hidden desires, my never satisfied hunger for affection and my unmitigated cry for God's mercy."[13]

Nouwen sometimes ascribed his longing for intimacy to effects of the parenting styles he experienced early on. Although he felt "enormous love" from his parents throughout his life, Nouwen also reported that in addition to his father's work-to-earn-love messaging, his mother was "a nervous, scrupulous woman whose many fears prevented her from freely holding and touching" him (*Home Tonight*, 36–37). It is likely that his parents, and his mother in particular, were influenced by Dutch childrearing practices of the 1920s and 1930s, which stressed a parental attitude of cleanliness, tranquility, and regularity (or, in Dutch, the "three Rs": *Reinheid, Rust en Regelmaat*). According to this regime, "feeding schedules had to be strict and infants were not to be picked up between feedings, for fear of spoiling them. Mothers were to let children cry until it was their suckling time and to refrain from cuddling. If possible, babies were to sleep in a quiet room undisturbed and alone. Older children had to obey, be polite, and were not allowed to disturb their parents."[14]

These rules of childrearing were likely very hard on Nouwen, who by all accounts was an intense and unusually sensitive child. The language for describing himself (especially before being edited) tended to be hyperbolic and melodramatic.[15] Being very sensitive was how Nouwen went through life.

The Loneliness of Celibacy

Long before he encountered the Rembrandt poster on Landrien's office door, striking that deep emotional chord, Nouwen had taken vows as a Catholic priest. Like all Catholic priests, Nouwen was a celibate. He was committed to his vows and experienced the practice as a "holy vacancy." In 1978, twenty-one years after taking his vows, he wrote,

The best definition of celibacy, I think, is the definition of Thomas Aquinas. Thomas calls celibacy a vacancy for God. To be a celibate means to be empty for God, to be free and open for his presence, to be available for his service. . . . I think that celibacy can never be considered as a special prerogative of a few members of the people of God. Celibacy, in its deepest sense of creating and protecting emptiness for God, is an essential part of all forms of Christian life: marriage, friendship, single life, and community life. . . . Every relationship carries within its center a holy vacancy, a space that is for the first Love, God alone. (*Clowning in Rome*, 43)

I believe that understanding Nouwen as a celibate is essential to understanding his response to Rembrandt's painting of the parable as documented in *The Return of the Prodigal Son*.

We learn more about Nouwen's position on celibacy from an article published in 2010 by A. W. Richard Sipe, a mental health counselor who spent eighteen years as a Benedictine monk and priest.[16] Sipe recalls Nouwen's reaction after hearing a talk that Sipe gave in 1991 called "The Celibate/Sexual Agenda." Nouwen wrote,

I also feel there is a dimension to the issue of celibacy that is absent from your presentation and, by its absence, gives your presentation an overly strong "political" character. Somehow I think that we really need to think more deeply about the mystery of communion and start talking in a new way about sexuality from there. I am certainly not yet able to do so and I find myself quite wordless around this very sacred area. But I do feel that we have to move beyond pointing to the many weaknesses and failures in living a credible sexual ethic to a rediscovery of the deep meaning of the "*vacare Deo*" [to be empty for God].[17]

Sipe continues with a recollection of a visit he had with Nouwen at Daybreak in 1991 that sheds further light on Nouwen's views. Sipe recounts that Nouwen's first occupations were the subjects of meditation and spirituality (he was reading Eastern meditation teacher Eknath Easwaran at the time). He then remembers that the second topic Nouwen wanted to discuss was celibacy and sexual orientation. Sipe writes, "Mainly his questions were about orientation. What really is it? Is it possible to alter it? What are the origins? What are its implications for celibacy? How does it affect spirituality? He was not quite at a point of personal resolution then." Sipe concludes, "Nouwen was the genuine article. He was exactly what he appeared—a priest struggling for integrity, exhausting himself in the service of others."[18]

Integrity is a word that is often used to describe Henri Nouwen. It is part of his appeal to so many people. The shadow side of integrity perhaps is scrupulousness that can pinch and dry out sensuality and the pleasures of physicality. By his own account, Nouwen wanted to avoid doing something wrong. In *The Return of the Prodigal Son* he confesses, "Since childhood [I] have scrupulously lived the life of faith" (*Prodigal Son*, 66). He shares with us that he feels a kinship with the obedient elder son who saw his younger brother flaunt what was expected of him to live a life of his choosing. "And all my life I have harbored a strange curiosity for the disobedient life that I didn't dare to live, but which I saw being lived by many around me" (*Prodigal Son*, 65).

We can only speculate what acts of disobedience tantalized Nouwen's fertile imagination; but surely one of them was how to live out his sexuality as a gay man. Nouwen was never public about his homosexual orientation, and after he died many in his close circle respected his choice. Biographer Michael Ford, however, decided to tackle the subject head-on. His biography *The Wounded*

Prophet (1999) took the thesis that much of Nouwen's insecurity and neediness was an extension of his unfulfilled homoerotic longings. While some consider Ford's biography to be too heavily focused on Nouwen's "wounds" at the expense of his qualities as a "prophet," he does have a point. Nouwen might have been able to accept celibacy as part of his priestly vocation, but it would have been harder to endure an internalized homophobia derived from the teachings of the Catholic Church.

Society's acceptance of homosexuality changed radically over the course of Nouwen's adult life, but in the early years of his career, homosexuality was generally seen as aberrant even in the liberal academic environments in which he circulated. The World Health Organization listed homosexuality as a health risk until as late as May 17, 1990. His father, like the majority of people in those years, thought that homosexuality was a disease.[19] Indeed, Nouwen himself wrote an article titled "Homosexuality: Prejudice or Mental Illness?" for the *National Catholic Reporter* in 1967 in which he argues for the latter.[20]

In the last year of his life, Nouwen described his views on homosexuality this way: "My own thoughts and emotions around this subject are very conflicted. Years of Catholic education and seminary training have caused me to internalise the Catholic Church's position. Still, my emotional development and my friendship with many homosexual people, as well as the recent literature on the subject, have raised many questions for me. There is a huge gap between my internalised homophobia and my increasing conviction that homosexuality is not a curse but a blessing for our society" (*Sabbatical Journey*, 27).

Nouwen's younger brother Laurent suggests that Nouwen sublimated his sexuality into religion; that his life, in fact, was "a battlefield between vocation and sexuality."[21]

As true as this statement might be, Laurent Nouwen would be the first to argue that it would be simplistic to reduce Nouwen's search for intimacy to one factor. This was, in fact, what Nouwen feared would happen if he engaged in public discourse on the subject. We can acknowledge its significance, but turn our attention to his stated search—his search for God.

Search for God

When Nouwen saw the poster he collapsed. At first, the reason for his strong reaction was pure exhaustion and a deep longing for his father's love. But gradually he began to see that the painting was actually a "large gate" for him to meet the One he had been searching for since he was born—"the God of mercy and compassion."[22] He found that the longer he looked at the painting, the more he saw that the image of God created by Rembrandt was not simply a friendly Father, but the womb of the divine Creator. He was returning to the womb, the seedbed of his true self. For these moments at least, his search for God was sated.[23]

Yet, his search wasn't over. When Nouwen's journey with the Rembrandt painting ended, another one began. In 1991, just as *The Return of the Prodigal Son* was entering the production stage with his publisher Doubleday, Nouwen became transfixed by another image of God. This time, it was a trapeze troupe called the Flying Rodleighs. In this group of creative people, Nouwen saw God as the catcher and us as the flyers who can take risks because of our trust that we will be caught. The full meaning of this image would take years for Nouwen to understand, but one facet of the attraction was its physicality. The trapeze-troupe image called Nouwen to consider his body and the physical aspect of the spiritual journey. It appears that the next leg of Nouwen's journey was to be a physical one. He was being called to enter into his body more fully. This is an important turn in Nouwen's life and one we will return to later in greater depth.

Henri Nouwen collapsed in front of the prodigal son poster in 1983. A number of factors, including his nature as a spiritual quester, led to that moment. When *The Return of the Prodigal Son* ends, we have witnessed a metamorphosis. A central event on the way was forgiving his father. He shifts his focus from the father he doesn't have to the father he does; and he finds freedom. He courageously lets go of the privilege of sonship and claims the gift of spiritual fatherhood. Nouwen senses the freedom of being a child of God without the prison of resentment or self-occupation. Blessing others becomes important.

As readers, we recognize this story because it shares elements of a hero's journey. Nouwen goes through trials and emerges on the other side a changed man. He lives his struggles differently in light of his newfound wisdom.

John O'Donohue, in his book *Anam Cara*, suggests that there is a place inside every one of us that has experienced God's unconditional love and that we spend our lives trying to get back to it. He writes, "We are capable of such love and belonging because the soul holds the echo of a primal intimacy."[24] Nouwen, through his personal story, tells this universal truth of life.

Chapter 2 ⁓
Intellectual Antecedents

Visio Divina *and the Spiritual Vision*

What you carry in your heart is what you see.

(Henri Nouwen)[25]

One might assume that the Rembrandt painting that struck Nouwen like a "lightning bolt" was a peak experience, a once-in-a-lifetime epiphany. In fact, Nouwen was on the lookout for "glimpses" of God at all times. As I noted earlier, he saw God in a trapeze troupe, for instance, and at the very time Nouwen was transfixed by "his painting," he was captivated by yet another image. This was a reproduction of a Rublev's Trinity icon, placed on the table in the room where he was staying in Trosly by Jean Vanier's secretary, Barbara Swanekamp. The Trinity icon, and other icons after it, became so connected with Nouwen's spiritual life that in 1987, five years ahead of *The Return of the Prodigal Son*, he would publish a book about them. That book, *Behold the Beauty of the Lord: Praying with Icons*, is important because it shows us how Henri Nouwen saw art and explains his capacity to enter so fully and fruitfully into the painting by Rembrandt.[26]

Behold the Beauty of the Lord was published in February 1987 by Ave Maria Press. It explores the power of looking at religious iconography in the Eastern Orthodox tradition and is structured around Nouwen's meditation on four icons and the meaning he found in them. As iconographer Robert Lentz pointed out in the foreword, it is not a scholarly work (though Nouwen prepared for the manuscript by reading deeply into the subject); it is a response of his soul (*Behold*, 11).

For Nouwen, icons allowed for transcendence without language and thought. He suggests that when we are tired, restless, or depressed, when we can't pray, read, or think, we "can still look at these images so intimately connected with the experience of love"[27] (*Behold*, 20).

In addition to helping us pray when we don't have words, Nouwen's book teaches us that we can *choose* what we see. We can take conscious steps to safeguard our inner space. Nouwen recognizes that we are bombarded with images, many of which are damaging, and we must be vigilant about where we put our attention. He writes, "It is easy to become a victim to the vast array of visual stimuli surrounding us. The 'powers and principalities' control many of our daily images. Posters, billboards, television, videocassettes, movies and store windows continuously assault our eyes and inscribe their images upon our memories. . . . Still, we do not have to be passive victims of a world that wants to entertain and distract us. We can make some decisions and choices" (*Behold*, 21).

Nouwen suggests that we commit images of art to memory, similar to how we might memorize the Jesus Prayer or passages from the Psalms. We memorize them to bring to mind when we need them. Nouwen, for instance, memorized work by Rembrandt and Vincent van Gogh. During his "Returning" retreat, he shared, "These Dutch painters have entered my heart in a very deep way, so I have them in my mind as I speak to you. They have become my consolation and when I find I have nothing to say, when I have only tears for what is happening in my life, I look at Rembrandt or at Van Gogh. Their lives and their art heals and consoles me more than anything else" (*Home Tonight*, 13).

When Nouwen was a child, the Nouwen family owned an original watercolor by Marc Chagall of a vase of flowers standing in front of a window. It was purchased by Nouwen's parents, Maria and Laurent, in Paris, shortly after their wedding and before Chagall's international fame. It hung in the family living room while Nouwen was growing up. Nouwen says that the painting, closely associated with his mother, who loved it very much, had imprinted itself so deeply on his inner life that it appeared every time he needed comfort and consolation. "With my heart's eye I look at the painting with the same affection as my parents did, and I feel consoled and comforted" (*Behold*, 19).

Visio divina, or "divine seeing," is an ancient contemplative practice that invites the practitioner to encounter the divine through images. Sharing roots with the practice of *lectio divina*—the practice of reading Scripture and then holding what one has read in the heart and contemplating it from there—*visio divina* is an interaction with an image to create a powerful experience of the divine. Practitioners of *lectio* and *visio divina* use the imagination to become each person in the story or image, to feel what they are feeling, to think what they are thinking, and to experience what they are experiencing.[28]

Visio divina as explained by Nouwen is more about gazing than looking. Instead of a kind of scrutiny, judgment, or evaluation, gazing is gentle, and allows for revelation. "Gazing," Nouwen explains, "is probably the best word to touch the core of Eastern spirituality. Whereas St. Benedict, who has set the tone for the spirituality of the West, calls us first to listen, the Byzantine fathers focus on gazing" (*Behold*, 22).

One day, Nouwen and his friend Sue Mosteller decided to go to the art gallery together. Nouwen was excited to show her a Vincent van Gogh painting of which he was particularly fond.[29] Nouwen bounded up the gallery steps and headed straight for the painting. It was in a small frame and depicted a field, trees, and flowers. Nouwen sat down on a bench in front of the painting and Mosteller sat down beside him. Nouwen stared at the painting with a look of deep concentration. Mosteller looked at the painting, too, but after a few minutes was ready to get up and move on. Nouwen, however, continued to gaze. Mosteller tried to see whatever it was that he was seeing. She examined the details one by one, the composition, the brushstrokes, but after a few minutes, she again grew restless. "Henri!" she finally said, "What are you doing?" Nouwen turned to her in surprise and said, "I am *in* the painting! I am in the South of France and it is so beautiful. Aren't you? Look at the colours! Look at the light!"[30]

This story allows us to speculate that Nouwen saw with a kind of spiritual vision. He could look at the world through the eyes of his heart, and perhaps even sometimes with the eyes of God. It was a practice he consciously cultivated. When Nouwen saw the little poster in Landrien's office, he didn't simply see a beautiful painting—he walked through the gate and into the outstretched arms of the father.

Nouwen was attuned to art through birth and culture. He was born in the land of the seventeenth-century Dutch masters, including Rembrandt and Johannes Vermeer, as well as famous Dutch painters of the nineteenth and twentieth centuries: Vincent van Gogh, Piet

Mondrian, and M. C. Escher. Nouwen would have been immersed in these paintings as a child and young man. As an adult, he felt a particular affinity with two of these artists: "I am a Dutchman, Rembrandt is a Dutchman and van Gogh is a Dutchman. . . . They are confrères" (*Home Tonight*, 13).

An Active and Developed Imagination

As well as exposure to great art, Nouwen had an active and developed imagination. We can enjoy pondering how differently he might have seen the world, as he walked through it, from the way we do. It calls to mind the story of his fascination with the trapeze troupe the Flying Rodleighs who were mentioned earlier.

While most people who saw the Flying Rodleighs perform at a circus enjoyed a beautiful aerial dance or a daring feat of athleticism, Nouwen, with his spiritual vision, saw God, the universe, and the whole meaning of existence. The trapeze act was yet another icon—this time an icon in motion—and it caught his imagination every bit as firmly as Rembrandt's painting. He wrote, "From the very moment they appeared, my attention was completely riveted. The self-confident and joyful way they entered, smiled, greeted the audience and then climbed to the trapeze rigging told me that I was going to see something—better, *experience* something—that was going to make this evening unlike any other."[31]

Nouwen first saw the Rodleighs while vacationing with his ninety-year-old father in Freiburg, Germany, in 1991. There was a peacefulness to the visit that flowed from Nouwen's lived experience of the Rembrandt painting. Nouwen reflected, "[Our] visit had about it that wonderful quality of mutual freedom and mutual bonding that can develop when both father and son have become elders."[32]

One day during the holiday, Nouwen saw a poster for the Circus Simoneit Barum. It was traveling through town, and they decided to attend a show. Sitting under the big top they enjoyed the animals and clowns, the juggling acts and tumblers, but it was the last act— that trapeze troupe called the Flying Rodleighs—that changed everything.

Nouwen was transfixed. Later, when he tried to articulate what it was that gripped him with such intensity, he had this to say: "The ten minutes that followed somehow gave me a glimpse of a world that had eluded me so far, a world of discipline and freedom, diversity and harmony, risk and safety, individuality and community, and most of all, of flying and catching."[33] He saw in this aerial dance an image that satisfied his lifelong desire to be totally free and totally safe. "I somehow caught a glimpse of . . . the mystery in which complete freedom and complete bonding are one and in which letting go of everything and being connected to everything no longer elude each other."[34]

Nouwen's ensuing trapeze obsession is an echo of his earlier experience with the Rembrandt painting. He asks, "Wasn't the ten-minute spectacle of these five people in mid-air like a living painting put together by great artists?" "Is this trapeze act perhaps one of the windows in the house of life that opens up a view to a totally new, enrapturing landscape?"[35]

Life Imitates Art

The trapeze act was such a vivid image for Nouwen in part because it resonated with his understanding of life as a vast canvas on which to draw our experiences. Like his confrère Rembrandt, who painted, etched, and drew more than ninety self-portraits in his lifetime, Nouwen wrote and rewrote his self-portrait through thousands of diary entries. He saw self-portraiture as a means to self-knowledge and a way to interpret his experiences. He made a practice of asking himself, "What did I do until now and where do I want to go?" He was always reviewing his life through the eyes of God and updating his portrait. He would encourage other people to "paint" their lives as well. Consider the phrasing he uses in a letter to a friend: "Your intuitions are so right and your basic orientation so valuable that a PhD might in the long run offer you the best frame to put your own painting in."[36]

Nouwen as Artist

Nouwen was attuned to art and artists because he was one himself. Perhaps more suitable than any other definition of who he was is the term "artist."[37] He used language and images to create meaning. Moreover, he saw his life as part of a larger story—God's story. Over and over, in his books, talks, and letters, Nouwen encouraged people to have a larger vision for their lives. In one letter to a friend he suggested the friend try to have "a Grand Canyon experience." He was referring to a time in his own life when seeing the Grand Canyon opened him up "to the mystery in which we are part." He said to the friend, "You too need a Grand Canyon experience."[38] We need to see our lives as part of something bigger than mere survival or worldly success.

Many of the insights in *The Return of the Prodigal Son* revolve around having a new vision such as this. Nouwen teaches us that when we act like the sons of the parable we cannot see properly. To clarify what I mean, let's review the Gospel of Luke chapter 15, where the famous parable of Jesus can be found.

A father has two sons: elder and younger. The elder son remains by the father's side, doing the work of a dutiful son, while the younger son asks for his inheritance so that he may leave; the younger son obtains the inheritance from his father and then leaves, squandering it all wastefully, eventually begging forgiveness and the ability to return to the father. When the younger son returns, the elder son questions his father, asking why he is so forgiving of the younger, wasteful one. The father replies, essentially, you have always been here with me, but he was lost and now is found.

Nouwen admitted myopia when stuck in the role of the elder son. He wrote, "When jealousy, resentment and bitterness have settled in my heart, I become unable to see what is already given to me. I am so focused on the seeming preference of God for the other that I completely lose sight of what is given to me."[39] Depression, he said, restricts vision, too: "I completely lose sight of the love that surrounds me, and no longer can see the reality as God sees it. Depression makes me see from below where I am and disables me to see from above where God is."[40]

Nouwen noted that Rembrandt, seemingly aware of the potency of the eyes of his characters, "chose to portray a very still father who recognizes the son, not with eyes of a body, but with the inner eye of the heart" (*Prodigal Son*, 89).

The Rembrandt painting became an icon for Nouwen, a gate through which he could walk into the house of God. But he could do that only because he had been practicing that kind of seeing for a very long time already.[41]

Anton T. Boisen and Henri Nouwen

Seeing Anton Boisen so closely and being able to experience how a deep wound can become a source of beauty in which even the weaknesses seem to give light is a reason for thankfulness.
(Henri Nouwen)[42]

When Henri Nouwen was asked in 1982 which people had most influenced him, he said Vincent van Gogh, John Henry Newman, and the people he ministered to.[43] He didn't mention Anton T. Boisen. This is not surprising. Boisen, the founder of clinical pastoral education in the United States, was the subject of Nouwen's keen interest and study for more than a decade between 1960 and 1970, but by 1982, he had moved on to other influences. Even so, it could be argued that there is no one who influenced Nouwen's life and work more than Boisen. Boisen, in fact, is in every fiber of *The Return of the Prodigal Son*. Yet, by the time Nouwen was writing it, Nouwen's use of Boisen was not conscious. He had built on Boisen's ideas, synthesized them, and made them his own.

Nouwen was likely first introduced to the work of Boisen by Willem Berger at the University of Nijmegen. Berger was a professor of pastoral theology while Nouwen was there working on his psychology degree.[44] At the time of his studies in the late 1950s and early 1960s, the Catholic Church in the Netherlands, after a period of outright rejection of Freud and others,[45] was moving into a position of nuanced support. In 1953, Pope Pius XII addressed participants of the International Congress of Psychotherapy with these encouraging words: "Be assured that the Church follows your research and your medical practice with her warm interest and her best wishes. You labor in a terrain that is very difficult."[46] Nouwen was in the vanguard of newly ordained priests choosing to study psychology rather than the more traditional disciplines of theology, classics, and languages. Under the influence of Berger and other leading Dutch thinkers such as Han Fortmann,[47] Nouwen chose Boisen as the subject for his doctoral thesis.

Nouwen would continue his work on Boisen when he moved to the United States to study in the program of theology and psychiatric theory at the Menninger Clinic in Topeka, Kansas, from 1964 to 1965.

After completing the program at Menninger, Boisen would also be the subject of a second doctoral thesis for an advanced theology degree at the University of Nijmegen.

When Nouwen joined the psychology department at the University of Notre Dame in 1964, his first academic appointment, Boisen was the subject of many lectures and was mandatory reading for students in his classes. Later, at Yale Divinity School, Nouwen's 1972 course on pastoral care also drew heavily from his work on Boisen. Boisen was, in fact, the subject of Nouwen's first book, one that he never completed, and of which no excerpts have ever been published. But, interestingly, Nouwen would not refer directly again to Boisen, the subject of so much of his attention for two decades, after 1977.[48]

In spite of Boisen's disappearance from Nouwen's life and work, evidence that he was a major influence can be found in the Nouwen Archives, where one finds shelves of material on Boisen. Over the course of his decade-long research and study, Nouwen visited the Topeka State Archives in the Kansas Historical Society to consult Boisen's papers and had all of Boisen's case histories mimeographed.[49] Included in this trove are fifty articles either on or by Boisen, many heavily annotated in Nouwen's hand.

The Clinical Pastoral Education (CPE) movement, founded by Boisen, began in the United States in the 1920s to educate ministers and chaplains for work in hospitals, psychiatric facilities, and other clinical settings. For adapting the clinical case study method that was introduced by Richard Cabot to the training of chaplains, Boisen is considered a pioneer of the case study method for pastoral care work. He developed a detailed methodology that was used in the process of gathering information about a person. Students using the assessment tool learned how to reflect systematically about the human condition, both psychologically and theologically.

A central tenet of Boisen's thought was that a person is a "living human document" on which experiences of life are written.[50] He taught that the same authority given to text should be given to the language used by those in mental struggles. In a speech to clinicians in 1950, he put it this way: "We are not trying to introduce anything new into theological curriculum beyond a new approach to some ancient problems. We are trying rather to call attention to the central task of the Church, that of saving souls, and to the central problem of theology—that of sin and salvation. What is new is the attempt to begin with the *study of living human documents rather than books*, and to focus attention upon those who are grappling with the issues of spiritual life and death."[51]

Boisen was born in 1876 in Bloomington, Indiana, to German immigrant parents. He graduated from Indiana University in 1897. Influenced by his father's passion for languages and nature, he taught French for two years in a Bloomington high school before earning a master's degree in forestry from Yale University in 1905. For three years he was a forest assistant for the US Department of Agriculture.

He started charting his own course at age thirty-five, enrolling in Union Seminary in New York City, where he was ordained a Presbyterian minister in 1911. Under the tutelage of Dr. George Albert Coe, Boisen began developing a view of the psychology of religion grounded in both religion and the study of human behavior. Boisen then served as both a Presbyterian and a Congregationalist pastor, was chaplain at the Iowa State University campus, and during World War I served with the YMCA in France. Like Nouwen, who also broadened his work experience by spending his postordination years in various religious settings, Boisen spent some time researching rural pastorates in Kansas and Maine as a sociological investigator for the Presbyterian Home Board of Missions.[52]

But none of this is the work he is remembered for today. In his late thirties, Boisen suffered a severe psychotic episode and required care in a mental hospital for catatonic schizophrenia. He suffered extreme bouts of psychosis for the rest of his life and was hospitalized in psychiatric facilities on numerous occasions. Using his own illness as a basis for understanding and expertise, he wrote much of his best work. Boisen would become the first chaplain at a mental hospital in 1924. He first worked briefly with the Boston Psychiatric Hospital, and then, with the help of Cabot, moved to the Worcester State Hospital in Massachusetts, and later to the Elgin State Hospital in Illinois. He eventually became a teacher, establishing the first program in clinical pastoral training in the United States, and helped found the Chicago Council for Clinical Training.

His first book, *The Exploration of the Inner World*, was published in 1936 and brought Boisen immediate international recognition. The book received critical acclaim in the *New York Times Book Review*, which identified it as "a significant contribution to the religious literary field."[53]

Boisen never married. The unrequited love of a woman, Alice Batchlaeder, whom he met in 1902 during his work with the YWCA in France, remained an obsession for most of his life. In his eighties, thirty years after her death, he still could not accept her rejection of him, calling her his "unreachable star." He died in 1965 in the Elgin State Hospital, near Chicago, at the age of eighty-eight. Few people attended his funeral. In the decades following Boisen's death, his legacy to clinical pastoral care and clinical pastoral education fell into relative obscurity. Today, however, several scholars are at work rehabilitating his seminal role in the development of these fields of study and practice.

A Visit with Anton Boisen

What accounts for Nouwen's sustained interest in this unusual man? And what does it reveal about the author of *The Return of the Prodigal Son*? Nouwen helps answer these questions through notes he left behind about a visit he made to Boisen shortly before Boisen's death. After years of studying Boisen, Nouwen visited him in person for the first time in August 1964. Boisen was eighty-six and a patient at the Elgin State Hospital. In notes written after his visit, Nouwen recalls the meeting as an intense experience. He expected impressive, solemn surroundings befitting the esteem in which he held his mentor, but experienced the opposite. After a long walk through gloomy corridors of the mental hospital, Nouwen was led into a little room behind the dining hall, where he found Boisen, disheveled and slumped in a wheelchair in a "poor, not very clean little room."[54] Nouwen asked Boisen about his influences (Freud). Boisen, in turn, was interested in Nouwen's identity as a Catholic priest and asked Nouwen about celibacy.

Intriguingly, Nouwen's final insights about the visit foreshadow themes of *The Return of the Prodigal Son*:

When I left I was very thankful that I had had the opportunity to meet this man whose suffering had become a source of creativity. The condition in which I found him showed clearly that his basic suffering never completely left him. Two years ago he had a new psychosis and he had lived since then on the borderline of reality. Especially when he became tired, the psychotic contents came more to the surface: his fear of a nuclear war, his many death-thoughts and his never completely solved love affair with Alice. He still idealized her who only wanted to be left alone and he still suffers from his puritanistic fear. But seeing a man so closely and being able to experience how a deep wound can become a source of beauty in which even the weaknesses seem to give light is a reason for thankfulness.[55]

This note contains a number of key insights into Nouwen and the reasons why Boisen was so significant in Nouwen's intellectual formation.

Let's take it a phrase at a time.

I was very thankful that I had had the opportunity to meet this man

Nouwen was thirty-two when he finally met the man he had been studying for so long. He expected "solemnity" but instead confronted a disturbing reality. Boisen was in a terrible state of neglect. Yet Nouwen was "very thankful." He could "see" something beyond his unmet expectations.

whose suffering had become a source of creativity

This might be the first time Nouwen contemplated the value of suffering that he so vividly articulates in *The Wounded Healer*. Boisen taught him to read "living human documents," and Nouwen's reading is that Boisen's suffering is linked to his creativity, to his insights. Nouwen links suffering with creativity. Suffering is a source.

his basic suffering never completely left him

This is crucial. Nouwen understands that suffering isn't always cured. What is required is that it is cared for, and from care, acknowledgment, and taking it out of the hidden places, the fruits of creativity and wholeness can grow. He allows himself the same compassionate response much later in his own life. In July 1996, he would write to a friend and describe his sexuality "as a great source of suffering" and an "unresolvable struggle," but he says, "I know that I do not need to be ashamed of my needs, that my demons are not really demons but angels in disguise, allowing me to love generously, to be faithful to my friends, to be sensitive to the many forms of human suffering and to live my priesthood with courage and confidence."[56]

never completely solved love affair with Alice

Boisen was open and honest about his unresolved sexual problems. In fact, he wrote about it extensively in early drafts of his autobiography, *Out of the Depths*, but his sister insisted on a less precise telling about this tender area of his life. Nouwen would have been struggling with sexual issues of his own. Is it too much to think that he would have understood Boisen's sexual preoccupations? What is significant is that Nouwen accepts Boisen without judgment.

his puritanistic fear

There are a number of striking similarities between Boisen and Nouwen. Both were the firstborn to educated, northern European parents. Both were ordained. Both worked in a variety of settings (trying to please their fathers) before settling into work that blended psychology and religion. Both were searching for a means of understanding their lives and struggles. Boisen, like Nouwen, was an academic but not in the conventional mode. He valued interdisciplinary study and innovation. Nouwen and Boisen are similar, too, in how they were not always taken seriously by academia because of their admission of vulnerability and weakness. Like Nouwen, even though he had not taken a vow of celibacy, Boisen remained single all his life. And here, too, in this reference to puritanism we see a similarity—Boisen and Nouwen both struggled with fear related to scrupulousness.

seeing a man so closely

Nouwen is visiting Boisen. He is listening to him, asking questions, and responding. He is also seeing him. He is looking at him closely. He is inviting intimacy with his gaze. Many in this situation would have shortened their visit, shied away from his infirmities, written Boisen off as too ill to contribute, and walked away disappointed and disillusioned. But Nouwen stayed. He looked at Boisen, and with this attention, he received the gift of insight.

a deep wound can become a source of beauty

This is the insight he received. Nouwen's deep compassion and his spiritual vision could see a wound, the wound of mental illness, as beautiful. This insight would travel with him for the rest of his life.

even the weaknesses seem to give light

Nouwen saw then, and forever afterward, that it is our weakness and vulnerability, specifically those aspects of ourselves that we want to keep hidden, that give the most light. Boisen was mentally ill, and yet it was from his illness that he drew his insights about pastoral care in mental institutions. Boisen gave Nouwen a model for radical vulnerability. He taught Nouwen to be courageous with his weaknesses, that sharing them would be a source of healing for himself and others.

a reason for thankfulness

Nouwen expresses gratitude at the beginning of his report and at the end. He knows that he has witnessed something life-changing. All his study and research had been leading to this moment when he could see with his own eyes, hear with his own ears, that Boisen's life was an expression of God. He understood that to live our lives well we need to unhook ourselves from the illusion of strength and claim our suffering, our struggles, our humiliations and failures. By doing so we can thrive and become sources of hope for others.

Boisen and The Return of the Prodigal Son

In seven important ways, Nouwen stood on the shoulders of Boisen while writing *The Return of the Prodigal Son*.

1. Using his personal story to tell God's story

Nouwen uses his own life as the basis for the book. He shares thoughts and feelings, many of which we might be more inclined to keep hidden, to connect the reader's experience with his own. He learned how to do this from Boisen and his case study method, but was likely equally inspired by Boisen's autobiography *Out of the Depths*, which was a classic example of using the study of a person as a primary document. Nouwen wrote, "His own case forms the core inspiration and his question was, 'What do these mental health disturbances mean for me, a minister who is trained in the psychology of religion?'"[57]

Similarly, we can imagine Nouwen asking, *What does this painting mean to me, a priest trained in the psychology of religion?* He might have also added, *What does it tell me about love?*

Nouwen used himself as the "living human document," but he also perfected the art of the case study of others. His earliest use of a case study, or biography, can be traced back to his study of Boisen. Much of Nouwen's thesis details Boisen's early life and formation. After the influence of Boisen, Nouwen used the case study method to understand Vincent van Gogh, another figure who was rejected in his lifetime as eccentric, even mad.

Like Nouwen, van Gogh was on a spiritual quest "to understand his place and purpose in divine creation."[58] Nouwen was a brilliant interpreter of van Gogh's paintings, but his real interest was in van

Gogh himself. His primary source of information was the painter's letters to his brother Theo. He read the letters to understand van Gogh's struggles, dilemmas, choices, and decisions. Through his reading, Nouwen saw van Gogh's gift of compassion. The letters were the primary documents for Nouwen's gaze into van Gogh's spiritual heart. He realized that van Gogh had a spiritual vision much like his own, that he was a "confrère" and his "saint."

Nouwen developed three courses at Yale around his interest in van Gogh, and even wrote a one-man play based on van Gogh's life in an effort to bring him to life for his students.[59] Van Gogh became a subject for his research and study, just as Boisen had.

Nouwen went on to apply the same "Boisen lens" to Thomas Merton, another fellow traveler whom he studied using the case study method. Nouwen's book *Pray to Live: Thomas Merton, A Contemplative Critic* (1972) was a biography that focused on Merton's life and work as a Trappist monk. Like Boisen and van Gogh, Merton was another seeker. Nouwen wrote, "He sought a place where he could feel at home, he sought an insight by which to bring order to the endless series of opposing ideas that poured over him in his various schools, and he sought after beauty that could give him the satisfaction he has fleetingly found in the many things that were presented to him as art" (*Pray to Live*, 39).

Nouwen was remarkably perceptive. John Eudes Bamberger, ocso, abbot of the Abbey of the Genesee and friend of Merton, would observe, "Henri Nouwen met Merton but once, yet by a sympathy of feeling and perception, he has understood the central motivation force of Merton's life: meditation and prayer. He has seen this more truly and profoundly than some who, while claiming to be intimate friends of Merton, have altogether missed the point of his work and life through lack of feeling for his vision of God, humanity and the cosmos."[60]

Nouwen applied this lens not only to mentors but also to his friends. The Nouwen Archives contains drafts of three biographies written by Nouwen that use the case study method. His friends Richard Alan White, a political activist; Lorenzo Sforza-Cesarini, a L'Arche assistant; and Stephen Jenkinson, an artist,[61] all became subjects of his attention. While only the Jenkinson piece was published (in *Image: A Journal of the Arts and Religion*, fall 1993), Nouwen's intent was to use biography to explore universal themes of the human condition.

Nouwen remained committed to the value of understanding our lives through stories. In 1994, he taught a course at Regis College in Toronto. The first assignment he gave his students was to write an essay titled "My History with God." He asked them to explore these questions: Where is God present in my life? Where is God absent? What brings me closer to God? What creates separation?

Finally, he used this lens on Rembrandt in *The Return of the Prodigal Son*. The insights Nouwen drew from Rembrandt's painting come more from his understanding of Rembrandt's tragic life than his brushstrokes or other elements of his technique.[62] Rembrandt began life as a very successful painter. He had children and a wife he adored. But then, he lost his beloved wife and four of his five children.[63] He lost his reputation and lived out his old age in poverty. He was buried as a poor man in an unknown grave. Nouwen writes, "[I] should not forget that it was Rembrandt's own story that enabled him to give [the parable] its unique expression" (*Prodigal Son*, 88).

He connected Rembrandt's suffering from the many losses in his life with his ability to depict the father in the painting as a man stripped of bravado and physical strength, a frail man who shimmers with mercy. The genius of *The Return of the Prodigal Son* is how masterfully Nouwen taps into the artist's poignant life story to shed light on how he could paint the family of the parable with such compassion.

2. *Reciprocity of "expert" and "patient"*

One of Boisen's key tenets is that the chaplain must confront and make peace with those parts of himself or herself that are mentally ill in order to be present to the patient.[64] In this sense, the chaplain becomes a fellow human being who by simply listening allows the patient to find his or her own answers. The mentally ill are given the chance to find their own meaning rather than merely being pathologized.

Boisen demonstrated and taught that there is a reciprocity in the relationship between chaplain and patient, between student and supervisor. The chaplain is not a detached observer but a participant, sharing vulnerabilities and learning from the patient in his or her care. By listening to the patient in a spirit of collegiality and cooperation, the chaplain learns more about his or her own story.

In a 1965 essay, Nouwen analyzed the medical model Boisen used in pastoral supervision and called it the "transparency of the struggle." By this he meant that Boisen modeled how to help people by using his own personal pathology as catalyst to help people in their own crisis. He taught theology students to read the living human documents of life experience, so when they graduated and became pastors, chaplains, and pastoral counselors, they were not just rote clinicians but companions.

Those who have read Nouwen's book *The Wounded Healer* will recognize here its central thesis. Nouwen may not have coined the phrase "wounded healer." (Possibly it was Jung, or it could have been even earlier; many myths and fairy tales present wounded-healer archetypes.) In any case, he is now, quite possibly, the most famous practitioner of this kind of reciprocal caregiving. In the book, he argues that ministers are called to recognize the suffering of their time in their own hearts and make that recognition the starting point of their service. Nouwen stressed that ministers must be willing to go beyond their professional role and open themselves as fellow human beings with the same wounds and suffering.

The power of *The Return of the Prodigal Son* lies in the fact that Nouwen uses his own struggles to find meaning and healing. He is a fellow pilgrim and not a detached expert with all the answers. He expects his readers to find their own path to reconciliation and freedom.

3. Trust in the wisdom of wounds

I suspect that part of what drew Nouwen to Boisen was what he did with his suffering. Boisen was on a quest to make sense out of his own experience and "to validate the meaning of the suffering that he went through in the midst of psychosis, self-flagellation and enormous internal conflict."[65] Boisen made creative use of his own psychosis. He acknowledged and used his vulnerability and weakness not as a narcissist or exhibitionist but because it freed others to tell their own stories.

Boisen taught Nouwen the value of illness as a way to health, which is what Nouwen explores with such transformational effect in *The Return of the Prodigal Son.*

4. Focus on the human-divine relationship

Nouwen's analysis of the painting and the parable of the prodigal son rests on the assumption of God's reality. Everything flows from this worldview. As a priest, Nouwen would have assumed this as self-evident, but Boisen's work helped Nouwen see that any understanding of himself, others, and God necessitated not just psychological study but a theological one as well.

For Boisen, chaplaincy work in a mental facility meant bringing the theological dimension into the circle of care. He believed it was the unique function of the chaplain to represent religion in all its aspects to the psychiatric team and to the patients. He taught that for healing to occur the chaplain must engage the human-divine relationship.

Nouwen would take this one step further. In an essay from 1965 on pastoral supervision, Nouwen argued that clinical training should use the mystical writings of Teresa of Ávila, Ignatius of Loyola, Thomas à Kempis, and Cardinal Newman to develop understanding of the human-divine relationship. He suggested chaplaincy students study the spiritual masters who "wrote thousands of pages about the stormy development of their most intimate relationship with God, with all its ups and downs, times of pain and times of rest, lives of understanding and intensities of darkness and light."[66] He concluded with an insight that would be recognizable to any reader of *The Return of the Prodigal Son*: "The spiritual life is a dynamic encounter with God."[67]

For both Boisen and Nouwen, one's own life story only makes sense within the larger story of God's creation. We don't live in a vacuum. We are part of a larger canvas. Our journey consists of understanding what our story reveals about us as much as it tells us about God and our divine-human relationship. Similarly, *The Return of the Prodigal Son* tells us as much about God as it does about Nouwen.

Boisen and Nouwen differed in one crucial way, however—how to relate God to the scientific method. Boisen pushed for a theology that documented the divine as an objective reality. Nouwen believed that there is something about the divine-human relationship that cannot be quantified. In *The Return of the Prodigal Son*, Nouwen's insights come from personal experience and feelings, and they are subjective. While they point to the divine and give us a "glimpse," they do not make God objectively visible. This argument for the

validity of the heart experience over objective thought is a tension
Nouwen lived with throughout his life. Boisen tried to bridge the
gap by using science for theology. Nouwen was less comfortable with
fitting God into a set of human-derived criteria.

5. *All problems stem from relationships.*

Boisen believed that the key to healing the person was healing
relationships, including the relationship with God. This emphasis
on relationships likely came from his own sense of loneliness and
isolation. Boisen and Nouwen were both in search of relationships
and used the search to help others heal and reconcile with significant
people in their lives. Boisen took this insight into the clinical setting,
and Nouwen integrated it into *The Return of the Prodigal Son*. Part
of what makes *The Return of the Prodigal Son* so compelling is the
attention Nouwen gives to the father-son relationship and that of
the brothers with each other. He then applies the same analysis to
his own life. The story pivots on his successful reconciliation with
his friend after his breakdown in 1987, and the forgiveness and love
he gives and receives from his father after his near-death experience
in 1989.

6. *Isolation as source of suffering*

According to Nouwen, Boisen's life work consisted of "discovering
ways in which [people] can overcome the sense of alienation."[68]
Nouwen understood this as Boisen's motive for the exploration of
his inner world. It is what brought Boisen through his wilderness,
which he calls "a little known country" and led him to his discovery
that "[romantic] love . . . can be truly happy only when [each person]
is a free and autonomous being, dependent not upon the other, but
upon God."[69]

"I believe," wrote Boisen, "that love is the paramount human need and that there is a law within which forbids us to be satisfied with any fellowship save that of the best religious experience, that is fellowship raised to its highest level, and religion is thus a necessary consequence of the social nature of humankind. From the religious standpoint, the aim of education is to lead the growing individual to transfer her loyalty from the finite to the infinite. For the religious person this higher loyalty is represented by the 'idea of God' and that idea stands for something that is operative in the lives of all humankind, whether they recognize it or not."[70]

Whereas Boisen would speak of transferring our loyalty from the finite to the infinite, Nouwen would speak of making clear distinctions between "first love" and "second love" to heal our sense of alienation. In an interview from 1989, Nouwen explains, "God loves us with a first love. John says, 'Love one another, because I first loved you.' The love of people is beautiful, but it's a reflection—a refraction, actually—of God's first love."[71]

He goes on: "The second love—whether it's friends, men, women, or community—cannot fulfill my heart. But I can be grateful for that love if I am deeply rooted in the first love. It means an enormous loneliness at times, a recognition that no human being is going to fulfill your heart, and you're really alone. But that is a good aloneness. Because that's where God speaks to you. That's a loneliness you have to nurture, instead of trying to get over it."[72]

Boisen and Nouwen were both searching for love. Boisen aimed to find a way out of the "little known country," and Nouwen wanted to leave "the distant country," as expressed in the parable. They admit to being lost but commit to finding a way forward. Their work has enduring meaning for us who also long to find a way out of our isolation and loneliness.

7. *Honoring the* imago Dei

It might appear that Boisen and Nouwen are overly attuned to human weakness, struggle, and suffering. Yet both Boisen and Nouwen honor the *imago Dei*, the unique "image of God" in each person God created. By recognizing God in the other and in themselves, they raise the human experience to noble heights. Together we can explore our condition in a circle of mutual respect. As divine beings, we can recognize the sacred quality of all we are living.

Chapter 3 ∽
The Writing Process

The reason for this book is to announce God's mercy
as the only and final response to our lostness.
—Henri Nouwen, about *The Return of the Prodigal Son*[73]

The seed was planted on a fall day in November 1983. But two years would pass before Nouwen's focus would again be riveted on Rembrandt's painting.[74] In those intervening years, Nouwen would move to Cambridge to teach at Harvard Divinity School, but his heart wasn't in the work. He enjoyed huge popularity for his "Introduction to the Spiritual Life" classes, but the exhaustion persisted. Something was not right. Nouwen would later reflect on the reasons for his unhappiness:

> It's too much podium, too much publicity, too public. Too many people came to listen. Plus Harvard is intensely competitive. It's not an intimate place. It's a place of intellectual battle. On the one hand, I loved being there. I made some beautiful friends. But, at the same time, I didn't feel it was a safe place where I could deepen my spiritual life.[75]

Eventually, the tension would become unbearable, and in July of 1985 Nouwen resigned from Harvard and returned to France to spend a year with Jean Vanier and his L'Arche community. In December, six months into his year away, he received a letter. It was from Daybreak, a L'Arche community in a suburb outside of Toronto, where he had just spent a few weeks during a brief North American visit. In the letter, Joe Egan, the community director, said, "We have something to offer you, and we have something to receive from you."[76] This invitation proved to be life-changing. Nouwen recalled that "it was the first time in my whole life that I felt called to anything. All the other times, I had made a lot of initiatives. But this time I felt God was calling me."[77]

In his letter back he responds,

> Let me start by thanking you for the beautiful way in which you and the Daybreak community have called me. This was clearly not a job offer, but a true call. It is the first time in my life that I have been so explicitly called. It was a real joy for me. I have often prayed: "Lord, show me your will and I will do it." Well your letter is an explicit answer as I probably will ever get to my prayer! . . . Reading your letter I had a real deep sense of a caring and loving community saying: come![78]

As he was preparing to move to L'Arche Daybreak he received yet another invitation. This one was from his friend Robert Kinloch Massie IV, a former student from Yale Divinity School.[79] Massie and his family were participating in a special tour of Russia—would Nouwen like to come along? Massie knew of Nouwen's long-standing interest in Russian Orthodox spirituality and culture, both through attending Nouwen's class on the subject and from Nouwen's long conversations with Suzanne Massie, Massie's mother, an author with a great knowledge of Russia. The tour would be with a group from the Orthodox Church of America, and its aim was to visit churches in the Moscow and Leningrad area as a lead-up to the millennium celebration of Christianity in Russia in 1988.

Massie recalls his telephone conversation:

> I said, "Would you like to go on this trip to Russia with us?" He called me back and he was just all a mess and he said, "I really want to go. I don't know if I can go but maybe, I think I do, hold a space, I probably can't. . . ." I had to call him two or three times which was unusual and I had to say, "Are you going or not?" He said, "Well, it's really an awkward time because I'm just going to move all my stuff and I've just promised them [L'Arche Daybreak] I'm going to be there for good and then I have to up and go." And I said, "All right, well then, don't go, don't come with us. That's fine." He said, "Well, no but I really want to go." And I said, "Then come." He said to me, "I would really like to be able to see the *Prodigal Son* [painting] at the Hermitage Museum."[80]

When Massie learned of how much Nouwen wanted to see the painting he called his mother Suzanne, who, with her deep connections to the arts community, was able to say, "Tell Henri he'll have as much time with the *Prodigal Son* as he wants."[81]

Nouwen joined the tour. Massie recalls that Nouwen was more tired than he had ever seen him. He fell asleep all the time. He forgot to eat. Massie recalls, "It was on the border of annoying because it was like having a five-year-old with you because he'd wander off and you'd have to say, 'Henri, come back, the bus is going to leave.'"[82]

But toward the end of the trip Massie noticed that, when Nouwen was finally able to visit the Hermitage, his demeanor changed. Massie remembers being with Nouwen when he first saw the painting:

I was not that taken with it. The truth is that . . . if Henri hadn't been passionately interested in it, I probably would have looked at it for thirty seconds and moved on to find something else a little more meaningful and attractive but he was really taken with it and approached it with a combination of reverence and curiosity. You know, looking at it, looking at it . . . he spent a lot of time with it. Now I don't remember how many times he went back. I know that he spent at least one four or five-hour block but I have this vague memory that he went back. We were off doing other stuff and he was sort of on his own track at that point and I didn't know where this was going to go.[83]

This encounter between Nouwen and Rembrandt, mediated through pigments and canvas, was not just research. It was a communication. It was as if the painting created a portal for a relationship that bridged time and space. Nouwen, who was so tired and discombobulated, was "in the painting," and my guess is he spent much of his time as the kneeling son absorbing his Father's unconditional love. Massie noticed that after each visit, "[Henri] came back with more energy, more light in his eyes. When we returned to the United States he seemed ready for the new life ahead of him."[84]

L'Arche Daybreak

L'Arche was a good fit for Nouwen. He became the pastor and was responsible for the spiritual life of the diverse community. A couple of years after arriving, Nouwen explained part of his attraction to the L'Arche way of life:

L'Arche has its own unique tone. It's not an institution. It's not a group home. It's a spiritual community where handicapped people are in the center. L'Arche exists not to help the mentally handicapped get "normal," but to help them share their spiritual gifts with the world. The poor of spirit are given to us for our conversion. In their poverty, the mentally handicapped reveal God to us and hold us close to the Gospel. That's a vision we have to nurture and deepen. I'm just beginning to discover it. I'm no expert on it. Nobody really is. But we live it very tenderly.[85]

Nouwen had found a community that embodied many of the values he'd been teaching. It was a place where he sensed he could grow and put down roots.

In other ways, Daybreak was more difficult than he expected. Sometimes he was like a fish out of water. He was in a place where no one was interested in what books he had written or what accolades he had accrued. They needed his help in the area in which he had the least skill and experience—the physical realm. He shared a house with several core members (as the people with handicaps are called) and their assistants. He was asked to help with meals, household chores, dressing and feeding of his core-member friends, and other routine daily tasks. He found these demands exhausting and sometimes wondered if this was the best use of his time.[86]

Living at Daybreak took a psychological toll as well. By the summer of 1987, his inner struggles came to a climax. The issue was his friendship with Nathan Ball, a young man whom he had met at L'Arche in Trosly. As Nouwen explains in *The Return of the Prodigal Son*, their friendship at the beginning had been mutually life-giving, but later, when they both lived at L'Arche Daybreak, Nouwen had gradually become obsessed with it. Ball began to feel claustrophobic and cut off all contact between them. Nouwen descended into a deep depression. It was decided he needed to leave the community temporarily and get professional help.

Reflecting back on this time in his life, Nouwen said, "Being among the handicapped people, I discovered my own handicaps, particularly with regard to issues of affection and friendship. As I lived longer in the Daybreak community old demons around my need for affection revisited me and I began to find it difficult to love freely without being selfish and demanding" (*Home Tonight*, 8).

On November 9, 1987, Nouwen moved to Homes for Growth in Winnipeg, Manitoba, a spiritual community and retreat center that offered therapeutic services for clergy.

"The anguish completely paralyzed me," wrote Nouwen in *The Inner Voice of Love*, the published diary of this episode in his life. "I could no longer sleep. I cried uncontrollably for hours. I could not be reached by consoling words or arguments. . . . All had become darkness. Within me there was one long scream coming from a place I didn't know existed, a place full of demons" (*Inner Voice of Love*, xiv).

It is worth pausing at this passage in Nouwen's life because much of what happened in his first years at L'Arche Daybreak becomes wisdom in *The Return of the Prodigal Son*. He was at Homes for Growth for nearly a year and received many different kinds of therapy, including holding therapy, and this had particular restorative power for him. Like the prodigal son, he was healed in part by the hands of his caregivers. In a letter from February 1988, Nouwen would write, "Jeanne and Jacques [his therapists] are true messengers of truth. They keep holding me with great faith and at moments that I feel like everything is coming to nothing they are there to free me from despair. They are gradually helping me to trust their love."[87]

Perhaps the most significant factor in Nouwen's recovery was the way he was held by the L'Arche Daybreak community. "Daybreak is your home and community," wrote Joe Egan one day to Nouwen. "I and the community carry you in our prayers and very much want to be a support to you. You must remind yourself daily that you are much loved by the people of Daybreak."[88]

Sue Mosteller, as mentioned earlier, played the key role in his restoration to health. Indeed, much of Nouwen's later contentment at Daybreak can be traced back to Mosteller. A woman of a similar age to Nouwen, she mentored and challenged him, while fully acknowledging his gifts. She modeled parental love that didn't need to be earned. She was his new "father figure," but of a very different kind.

Originally from Akron, Ohio, under the influence of her Canadian-born mother, Mosteller entered the congregation of the Sisters of St. Joseph Toronto in 1952 after high school. She taught for fifteen years, during which time she completed a degree in English at the University of Toronto, graduating in 1968. In 1967, she met Jean Vanier and by 1972 had joined the L'Arche Daybreak community. In 1976, Mosteller was elected to replace Jean Vanier as the international coordinator of L'Arche, a position she held for nine years before resuming her life at Daybreak. During her time in the position, the L'Arche network expanded from thirty-five to sixty-five global communities.

Nouwen first met Mosteller in the 1980s at a conference. For the next few years they exchanged letters to keep in touch. When Nouwen visited Daybreak in 1986, he impressed the community with his pastoral skills after a core member was involved in a near-fatal accident. It was Mosteller who, seizing on an opportunity to invite him to live with the community on a more permanent basis, helped draft the letter of invitation that changed the course of his life. She emphasized that Daybreak was "calling" Nouwen to the position, very likely the key reason he responded with such enthusiasm. In addition to a home, he was looking for and needed to feel a vocational call.

To Mosteller, Nouwen would write on February 18, 1988, about his relief that he was at Homes for Growth. He mentions Jean Vanier, who had assisted in finding a good place for his care:

I cannot tell you how much it means to me that God has given you to me to affirm in this conviction. It is such a grace that I do not have to fight to make you or Jean [Vanier] believe that I am at the right place. It is also a great grace that during the hours of doubt and questioning and during the moments I want to run away in distraction, you and Jean are there to remind me that it is truly God who has called me here to be with him alone. It is a very awesome awareness and full of grace.[89]

In another letter to Mosteller from February 1988, he wrote,

I pray for you with much love. I know how much you have struggled and suffered because of me, but here I do not feel guilty or ashamed! I really believe that our friendship, your friendship with Nathan and me, the Dayspring [Daybreak's chapel and spirituality center, where Mosteller, Nouwen, and others shared a home] and all that has happened since your move there, are part of a mysterious plan of God that one day we will be able to recognize. The grace that I am not alone in this time of anguish and that you know me so well and so compassionately, is so great and so marvelous, that I cannot thank Jesus enough for it. And I know that this grace, with all its ramifications, will radically affect our lives. I am glad that I cannot look into the future! But I know that we both will see everything in a new way because of what we are living now.[90]

Mosteller recalls what Nouwen brought with him to Winnipeg: the things he needed to perform the Eucharist and a copy of the poster of Rembrandt's prodigal son painting. After intensive therapy sessions, he would retreat to his room and meditate on the painting—

feeling, as he did the first time he saw it, that it was a place of refuge from "the anguish of abandonment" (*Prodigal Son*, 45).

He started to put down his thoughts about the painting in late 1987. He writes, "So, as I am sitting in this small room far away from L'Arche, trying to live through the experience of being completely lost, . . . I want to write about this painting and the story it portrays."[91] Eventually, he had a short draft. Mosteller received a copy to review. She wrote a letter of response on February 28, 1988:

> The reflections you sent on the Prodigal Son were good. I've read them several times. . . . The reflection I make springs from your writings on the PS but is primarily NOT for the text that you sent me. What I want to say is for you and for your life today, where you are.
>
> I believe so much that picture was given to you, first for your life and perhaps later for your writing, and I also believe that at this particular moment something is being given to you because of it. You have really "found yourself" more deeply there than anywhere. You long to make the passages called for from each of the sons, ie. to come home to your Father's house with the younger son and to move from resentment to compassion with the elder brother. In coming home you claim your sonship to the Father which is to claim a part of your identity. But with the passage of the elder brother you are choosing another aspect of your identity, namely your brotherhood with the rest of the human family. You begin to KNOW who you are from a very deep place and you begin to claim it and to stand up and to live from there. I guess I just want to ask you if, in fact, you are not almost there?
>
> You have made some very deep and significant choices to grasp and live from your centre where you know that you

are unconditionally loved even if you don't feel it. I expect that even when you leave Winnipeg you hope to be able to hold onto that choice. It is THE choice which connects you with your Father. In that choice you are home. And you are certainly not wanting to live from resentment in front of God, your family, Nathan, or others who have been and are significant for you. You want to love and you want the good of the other even if you are not able to give it. In that choice you are passing from resentment to compassion. These choices you have taken already. In actual truth you are not longer the errant son or the elder, angry brother because of the fact that something there has been chosen and rectified at least in your heart's desire if not always in your emotions and feelings. So yes, I believe that in your desire, at least, you are home.

But I have also been asking myself who the Father is. You describe Him so well. It is obvious that He is our Father, God. But perhaps there is something else here to think about yourself.

As I see you over these past years and months I ask myself if the real call for you is the call to become the Father. Once the sons have made their unique passages are they not then ready to become like the Father, to become the Father? And truly Henri, aren't you right there? Is that what this passage is all about? Isn't this why you chose to come to Daybreak in the first place; because in your life journey you were more ready to be Father and you knew somewhere in yourself that it was time to "put away the things of the son"?

I can see this call for your rising up from within yourself, the call to become Father. Isn't your heart burning within you to be able to love others as that Father loves? Wouldn't you find a deep sense of fulfillment to be able to be here in this community as the Father was in his own home? Here you would be in your home and you would wait patiently for the errant ones to come home and you would accept and hold onto the resentful ones until they were ready to make their own passage. Does this make any sense to you?

I could go on but I don't want to go too far until I hear your reactions.

But isn't it this that draws you in your relationship with Père Thomas and with Jean?[92] In some sense they too have made the passages of the two sons, but now are they not both Fathers, like that Father? Do you feel at all drawn to that?

And I could say that the call for you here is exactly that. We need you to come back and to be Father here. In that call, because you are not God, the Father, you will continually meet the sons who are in you and you will have to choose to stay home and to overcome your resentment.

Perhaps this time in Winnipeg is there to help you to see that you have to choose to BE home, but to be home as Father more than as son.[93]

Nouwen responded,

March 4, 1988

Dear Sue,

Thanks so much for your wonderful letter about the Prodigal Son. It really holds a very important challenge for me. Frankly, I have thought about what you said a little bit in the past, but always with some hesitation. There has been in me such a need to become a brother that becoming a father always frightened me. Still, I very clearly see the great call that is implied in your letter and I even believe that when I would be able to claim my fatherhood, many of my needs to be accepted and loved by people who are much younger than I am may be transcended. I am very glad you raised this very important issue and it certainly belongs to my spiritual journey in years to come.

I am very sure that I can only truly become a father if I have also been a real brother and it seems quite a spiritual task to become brother and father within a short time. Still, I really believe that both challenges, of becoming a brother and of becoming a father, are becoming increasingly a part of my struggle here at Homes for Growth. It is exciting to think about this more as I pick up again the work on the Prodigal Son. Thanks so much for your insights, inspiration and challenge.[94]

In early summer, after eight months at Homes for Growth, Nouwen began to consider returning to Daybreak. His therapists felt he needed more therapy, but Mosteller was convinced that he was ready to return to community life. The question was, could Nouwen return to Daybreak if Nathan Ball was still there? Ball was the community leader now. Could they live and work together again? It was decided that Nouwen would make a short and contained visit in July with an aim of a complete return in the fall. Mosteller prepared the way for Nouwen and also for Ball:

July 12, 1988
Dear Nathan and Henri,
You both know how much I love you and carry you in my poor old heart! I want to support you in your lives, especially

in your call to live at Daybreak. Because of that I become bold—to presume to have something to say to you at this moment. It is *in* me and so I share it with you.

I have been praying for and about your meeting for a long time and I am praying for you today.

I hope that you will be able to recognize and rejoice in the fact that each of you is choosing to meet the other. Please see this as gift and a grace. Recognize that God's Spirit is present there.

And what you are doing is not something just between the two of you. You are concerned about our world and our Church and about the divisions everywhere that are cause of such deep and profound sufferings. I believe that all that is contained in what you are being asked to live between you. We want the North and the South to meet and to listen to each other and try (once more) to live together on the planet and to love one another. We want Iran and Iraq to try to dialogue, to listen to see how to be neighbours. We want the Palestinians and Israelis to recognize and accept and love one another—to give each other space—a home, so as to live and grow. We want churches to remember and welcome membership in the Broken Body of Jesus. And we want all those men and women in families and with their children to strive for the way of peace. Is this not the context of your meeting each other? You too, seek a way of love.

I want to confirm each of you in the love you have for the other. I also confirm you in your love for God and for His call to you to be men of love and peace.

I ask you to remember two important truths:

You cannot understand what is happening, nor the reason for the pain you are asked to live in your relationship. You must not ask for it. You cannot fix it or make it work yourselves. You know it. It's OK though. Just accept and claim your fragility, your poverty.

God will give you a new force. You CAN trust that and ask for it and act from it. God will give you ears and a heart to hear and receive what the other has lived, and suffered. God will give you space to hear the truth of the other.

And God will give you the force to announce your truth to each other. There is hurt and brokenness, pain and sorrow which must be shared and received. With God's force you will hear it in a new way. Please trust that—and listen, and speak from the place where that force is given in you.

I beg you, my brothers to be very careful and gentle. Today is only one little step. Try NOT to have expectations of each other. That prevents you listening. God will be with you. You can trust Him to show you how you must walk forward. We need you to do this—Daybreak, L'Arche, The Church, The World. So much can flow from your acceptance of the pain of the breakage and your trust in the God of love.

I love you, I trust you and commit myself to walk with you in His love,

Sue[95]

Henri Nouwen left Daybreak and then he returned. With the help of Mosteller, and his own commitment to finding a way to share community life together with Nathan Ball, he was able to return. Not as the prodigal son, but as an important part of the community. He was welcomed home.

The painting was his lifeline. When he first saw it at L'Arche in France, when he sat for hours in front of the original at the Hermitage in Saint Petersburg, when he meditated with his rolled-up reproduction in his little room in Winnipeg, when he returned to Daybreak, the painting offered him a way of hope through his pain. It was only after he had plumbed the depths of his anguish that he could finally begin the process of putting words around what it said to him.

The First Draft

As mentioned, Nouwen first began to write about the prodigal son in 1987 while he was at the Homes for Growth. As he struggled to articulate what the painting was saying to him, he wrote, "The reason for this book is to announce God's mercy as the only and final response to our lostness."[96]

Nouwen had preached on the parable every year since his ordination, but he was seeing something new in the way Rembrandt portrayed the father and the kneeling son. It connected with something very deep within himself. Nouwen would write,

> Rembrandt had understood something that belonged to my most intimate search. It is the search for a love beyond insight, beyond words of recognition, beyond any declaration of affection, a love that exists long before it can be understood, appreciated and returned. My life journey— as long as I can remember—has been a journey of search for a "blind and silent love," a love that did not look at how I was clothed, nor depended on my words of repentance, a love that whispers to my heart: You are accepted, you are desired; from all eternity. "See, I have engraved you on the palms of my hands"(Isaiah 49:16).[97]

This 1987 Homes for Growth manuscript, the first draft of *The Return of the Prodigal Son*, is thirty-six double-spaced pages. There is only one copy of this manuscript extant. It came to the Nouwen Archives through a donation of material from Gordon Turner, a United Church minister. From a cover letter to Turner from Nouwen's secretary Connie Ellis, it appears Nouwen wrote the manuscript in preparation for a talk to university students. Ellis wrote, "Enclosed are the notes Nouwen used for his talk at Regis College [University of Toronto]. He asked me to stress to you that these are just notes, not a manuscript. He does hope to work more on them and perhaps produce a manuscript later, but at the moment they are not nearly ready for any kind of publication. He is sending them to you as an interested friend and is happy to do so, but, of course you will understand that he would not want them distributed in any way as a finished piece."[98]

Ellis concludes by referring to Nouwen's absence from Daybreak. "He really does not yet know when the state of his health will permit him to return." We are reminded of Anton Boisen, who made his more significant contributions while struggling with his own mental-health issues in a psychiatric hospital.

In June 1988, while still living at Homes for Growth, Nouwen built on his ideas by leading a six-day retreat for L'Arche assistants. It was his second public effort to express what the painting meant to him.[99]

The first full-scale manuscript then began in 1989, when he was settled back at Daybreak. He wrote a letter to the Daybreak council on January 20, 1989, requesting a leave to write:

Dear Friends,
During the past months, I have become increasingly aware of my great need to start writing again. I am, therefore, writing

you with a proposal that I spend a few months in Europe to focus exclusively on writing the book on the Prodigal Son which has been emerging in my mind and heart over the past several years.

Let me give you some background to clarify my situation. As you know, from the very beginning when I came to Daybreak I have been encouraged by you, as well as by many others in the community, to continue to write, and I have always felt strongly encouraged by the community to consider writing as a real vocation and something I should not give up in joining L'Arche. However, during the past three years I have become increasingly aware of how hard it is for me to do any in-depth and systematic writing while being actively involved in the daily life of the community. This is not because the community asks too much of me, or because my writing is not appreciated, but because I have not been able to find the inner rest and space that is necessary for writing that is more than articles or short meditations. I have tried very hard to find some inner and outer space and time to write while at Daybreak, but so far I have failed in doing that well.

Meanwhile, my stay here has been extremely fruitful in terms of new ideas and new visions. Living at Daybreak has really stimulated my heart and mind very much, and presently I feel filled with ideas and insights that want to be expressed in literary form. Especially the Parable of the Prodigal Son and the portrayal of that parable by Rembrandt have increasingly emerged as a way to give expression to many of the things that I have lived here. During my stay in Winnipeg, I was able to collect most of the material, material on Rembrandt as well as material on the parable, but since I returned in September I have not really had any time to work on this project. It is the kind of project that requires long days of solitude and silence and many hours to give structure to the kind of book I have in mind. And as the time progresses, I start feeling a certain fear that I am losing touch with my material and that it becomes harder and harder to realize the project that I have been holding in my heart for so long. At this time, I really do not know how much time I need to do the kind of work I have to do, but I have a deep sense that it is important to not feel any time pressure. Usually, I need a few weeks to simply get into the right spirit and do some preparatory reading, and after it is still often a real struggle to find the right composition and structure that make a major book.[100]

Nouwen proposes that he travel to Freiberg, Germany, where he would live with the Sisters of Mercy and write in the home of the Herders, friends and owners of his German publisher Verlag Herder. He hoped he could work on the book during April and May and consider the month of June as a month of vacation, "which I could use to write if I had not got far enough by then."[101]

It was important for Nouwen that his writing, especially on the prodigal son, be connected with his membership in the L'Arche Daybreak community. He continued,

I realize that being away from the community for such a long time has many drawbacks and might even make some people wonder if I am fully committed to the life here. I also realize that some members of the community might not feel that I can fully exercise my ministry here when I am not constantly present. But the more I reflect on my vocation, the more I feel that no longer writing would eventually be harmful, not only for me personally, but also for me as a pastor for the community. I would very quickly become dried up and have no longer the kind of vitality that comes from times of reflection, reading and writing. Looking at my vocation as a whole, I deeply believe that writing cannot be truly important if I only can do it when there are no other important or urgent things asking for my attention. In order to do the kind of writings that I have in mind at this moment, it seems essential for me considering my own character and desire to be involved in the community, to take a radical step away and to create an atmosphere for myself in which morning, mid-day and evening I can be totally absorbed in my subject and have no temptations around me to pay attention to anything else. . . . I am deeply convinced that my writings about the Prodigal Son is for L'Arche and for Daybreak, and is only possible because of my being part of this community. Going away, thus, is not a going away to do my own thing, but going away in order to be a fruitful member of L'Arche and to offer the community the best of my gifts.[102]

But despite his best efforts Nouwen wasn't able to get away as hoped. He was needed at Daybreak. In a letter to a friend he writes of his disappointment but also of his continuing enthusiasm for the project:

Thank you for your very encouraging words about my writing. Regretfully, I have had very little time to write over the past few years, but I keep hoping that I can return to it in the near future. One of my dreams is to write a book about the Prodigal Son in close connection with the painting of that scene that Rembrandt made at the end of his life. I have collected all the material, but have not yet had the kind of space I need to start putting things together. Somehow, I feel it is a theme in which I can best express my own spirituality.[103]

Time to write finally came in January of 1990. He was able to clear his schedule and flew to the Trosly community in France. In two months, he was able to complete the first draft he had started at Homes for Growth three years earlier.[104]

The European Edition

While in Europe, Nouwen spoke with his close friend and editor Franz Johna about his plans to write a book about the painting. Johna was the editor for Verlag Herder and began giving Nouwen resources and ideas to support the project. Nouwen also spoke to Lieven Sercu, the editor of the Dutch publishing firm Lannoo. Lannoo had already published most of Nouwen's previous books. Sercu received the idea for his book with equal enthusiasm. Both his Dutch and German publishers agreed to publish based on a reading of the first draft.

Nouwen also sent his first draft to William (Bill) Barry of Doubleday in New York. Nouwen had already published ten books with Doubleday and had worked with Barry on many of them. Barry was a seasoned editor with a career that began in 1979, when he joined Doubleday's religious imprint Image Books as an editorial assistant.

Doubleday was one of seven publishers that Nouwen had worked with up to that point. Founded in 1897 as Doubleday and McClure Company, by 1947 it was the largest publishing house in the United States. Other authors in the elite stable of writers for Doubleday in the 1990s were Isaac Asimov, Margaret Atwood, John Barth, and Wallace Stegner. Today, Doubleday is part of Penguin Random House, which is in turn owned jointly by German media giant Bertelsmann and British education publisher Pearson PLC.

In late spring of 1990, Nouwen sent the manuscript to a few friends: Esther de Waal (a family friend and author on the Benedictine tradition), Sue Mosteller, James Purdie (*Globe and Mail* art critic),

and Brad Colby and Glenn Peckover (two friends from Daybreak).
Each expressed that it was a fine work and close to completion. Sue
Mosteller was prescient in her evaluation. She wrote,

> The Prodigal Son manuscript is in my humble option, not only
> your best book so far, but also, a classic. It captures something
> so universal and so profound that it is truly a book for every
> person. I cannot thank you enough for having lived it first
> with such consciousness and now have written it with such
> power and gift of expression. It is a fabulous book, exciting,
> daring and rich. This I am certain must be the reaction of
> many future readers![105]

Having received these responses, Nouwen held a meeting in
Toronto on May 8, 1990, to discuss his first draft further. De Waal
(visiting from England), Mosteller, Elizabeth Buckley (one of his
housemates and member of Daybreak), Conrad Wieczorek (an editor
Nouwen hired to do substantive and fine copyediting), and Connie
Ellis, his trusted secretary, were all present. Again, the response was
positive.[106]

The book contract with Doubleday was signed on August 23,
1990. Nouwen retained foreign rights for Dutch and German editions
and secured a $65,000 advance against future royalties. Today, this
amount would represent approximately $120,000. His Dutch and
German editors were already well along in the book's production.
They planned for a release date of October 1991 to coincide with the
Frankfurt Book Fair. Johna wrote on September 11, 1990, that he
had read a revised draft of the manuscript that Connie Ellis had sent
him: "The building of the story is lovely and builds to a harmonious
conclusion."[107]

Publication and Initial Reception

In September of 1990, Nouwen really began to concentrate on completing a final draft. However, this was not his only writing project in the works at that time. In 1990, *Walk with Jesus* and *Beyond the Mirror* would be published. Writing was also underway for *Life of the Beloved: Spiritual Living in a Secular World.*

He was a busy man. In a letter to Bill Barry at Doubleday, September 10, 1990, written after a visit by Barry to Daybreak, Nouwen wrote, "I regret that my time is so limited and that the work in my community is so intense that I can't work as fast as I had hoped, but I am happy that you know our situation at Daybreak a little bit and can identify with it."[108]

Not mentioned in his letter is that, for most of early 1990, he had been recovering from the near-fatal accident that occurred in November of 1989. This event precipitated a cathartic conversation with his father that would prove to be pivotal for *The Return of the Prodigal Son*. Nouwen needed to claim fatherhood for himself before he could write about it for others. Mosteller had already alerted Nouwen to this blind spot after reading the first draft from 1987 while Nouwen was still at Homes for Growth.[109] In the 1990 draft he had still not fully worked out how to effect the transition from son to father, let alone describe it. Mosteller would write,

> I simply do not feel that you are claiming where you are today, and for me, that not only weakens considerably your message, but it also rings a titch untrue at times. Obviously, I do not accuse you of being dishonest, but rather want to ask you to claim the truth of where you actually are today. My sense is that you really have to do it in order to authentically ratify the truth of the parable. This may require an inner clarification which you may fear, but truly I do not think it matters where you say you are, as long as you claim your truth and write from there.

. . . Only you know about where you are on this journey towards identification with the Father. I am asking you to claim that place with all its struggle and also with all its beauty and fulfillment. I am convinced the parable is so meaningful because you have found yourself almost everywhere in the younger and the elder son's experience. My sense is that you are living an experience of the Father that you perhaps, are not willing or confident enough to claim. I suggest that for the manuscript to, not simply enlighten, but to be an instrument to confirm others where they are and to call them to claim the truth of where they are, you must somehow cross over and risk to claim your true situation in all its authenticity.[110]

By December 1990 the final draft was nearing completion. Details started to get more attention. One was the masculine quality of the language. Nouwen was concerned it would alienate women. To Barry he wrote, "Since the book is about a father and two sons, and since the author is a man too, the language is very masculine. Would this make the book somewhat exclusive of women? I have discussed motherhood of God on pg. 145 and following, but the overall language continues to be very masculine language." Barry decided Nouwen had done enough to make the book inclusive.[111]

Another detail that concerned Nouwen was how the Rembrandt plates would be reproduced in the published book. Nouwen wanted the same quality as he'd seen in another book he admired (*Paintings from the Soviet Museum*), and went so far as to suggest Doubleday may have to send someone to Saint Petersburg (then Leningrad) to photograph the details he needed. He also began to consider his author photograph. He offered the name of an artist-painter friend, John Brocke, who had recently completed portraits of him.

Nouwen sent the final manuscript to Barry at Doubleday on January 17, 1991, writing, "I hope you will give special attention to the aesthetic aspects of this publication so that it will reflect the beauty of the painting on which it is focused."[112] In February, the issue of the book title came up. Thus far, the book had three working titles: *A Dreadful Mercy*; *A Dreadful Love*; and *Canvas of Love*. Barry wrote with a number of new suggestions, including *The Prodigal*; *The Parable of the Prodigal Son*; *There Was a Man Who Had Two Sons*; and *The Return of the Prodigal Son*. For a subtitle he offered: *On Becoming the Father*; *A Father's Love*; *A Story of a Father's Love*; *A Parable of Fathers and Sons*; *A Parable of Discovery*; *A Parable of the Father's Love*; and *The Welcome of the Compassionate Father*.

Nouwen responded, "'Father and Sons' is too masculine, 'Prodigal Son' is too archaic, it isn't a modern word. I still like Canvas of Love the best." One month later, he added,

> While flying to Holland, I thought a lot more about the title
> of the book, and I simply want you to know that I, personally,
> find Canvas of Love a very good title. It is short and it really
> tells what the book is about. The book is about love in its many
> shades and forms and about a painting. The whole purpose of
> the book is that this canvas of love become an interior image
> that people can continually use in their personal growth. . . .
> The word "canvas" refers to a painting and the word "love" to
> relationships; together they might create more interest than
> would the words "prodigal son" which tends to identify it as a
> strictly religious book.[113]

A discussion about the release date quickly followed. Doubleday wanted the book released in May 1992 in anticipation of Father's Day promotions in June. Nouwen disagreed:

I still am not totally in touch with the argument that publishing it around Father's Day is better than publishing it before Christmas. In many ways I think it would be such a good book to read in the Christmas season and that it would respond better to the spiritual meaning of it than making it connected with quite a secular Father's Day. Although the book speaks about God the Father a lot and about spiritual fatherhood, I find it somehow superficial or even trite to try to connect that spiritual truth with a day that is so much the fruit of commercialism.[114]

Differing visions continued. In September 1991 Nouwen penned a letter to Barry about erroneous information on the back cover. ("L'Arche Daybreak is not the headquarters of L'Arche, and it would be very upset to be labeled as such.") Then in January 1992, Nouwen wrote that he was disappointed in the cover design: "I think it should be personal and very emotive, soothing and evocative." Nouwen wanted the book to have the same design as the Dutch and German editions. Their release date was earlier than the American edition, and Nouwen was pleased with the cover design and overall quality of the reproductions.[115]

The North American hardcover edition came out as planned by the Doubleday team in May 1992 in time for Father's Day in June. The book was designed by Richard Oriolo, a freelance book designer from New York who had studied at the School of Visual Arts. Nouwen's concerns with the masculine and archaic quality of the title were not addressed. It was published as *The Return of the Prodigal Son: A Meditation on Fathers, Brothers and Sons.*

Between June and October 31, 1992, it sold 8,727 copies, a very good first quarter. Such initial sales were a solid start for Doubleday, but not one that would have foretold the popularity of the book to come.

The people who bought and read the book were enthusiastic. Six months after its release, Nouwen wrote to Barry, saying that he was getting a very positive response to the book and hoped there would be another print run for Christmas 1992. He told Barry that he had lined up Robert Schuller, the *Hour of Power* televangelist; Mary Rourke, a staff writer for the *Los Angeles Times*; and Steven Berry, a minister at the First Congregational Church of Los Angeles, to help him promote it. Nouwen wanted the book advertised in a "few major magazines" and mentioned Madeleine L'Engle's *Certain Women* and the fact that it got a full spread in the *New York Times Book Review*. He hoped he could get the same treatment, since he and L'Engle were on the "same wave length." "It is unusual for me to be so pushy around my books, but with this book I find it different than any other book. I am confident that this book is my very best book and that it can speak deeply to people at this time. The letters and phone calls that I receive are too convincing to doubt that."[116]

It was true; reader response to the book was strong. Critical response was also good, but it did not lead to many reviews, as Nouwen had hoped, and especially not by more secular publications like the *New York Times*. To get a better perspective on reader and critical response, it would be useful to look at the historical context in which *The Return of the Prodigal Son* was published.

Some Historical Context

The Return of the Prodigal Son was published in May 1992. While this first release into the world was an important moment in the life of the book, in Nouwen's life it was one event among many. Nouwen's personal life was moving ahead at a fast clip. In some respects, he had moved on.

The year that began with his memorable clown birthday also saw a renewed mandate as chaplain at Daybreak for an additional four years.

It was granted after a substantial review of his contribution to the Daybreak community. Jean Vanier and other reviewers noted, "We feel that Jesus has really called Henri to be a priest for Daybreak. We rejoice and give thanks for all that has been accomplished."[117] His bishop, Cardinal Simonis, was also convinced that Daybreak was the best place for Nouwen to live out his ministry. Feeling the support and confidence of the community elicited a surge of activity in Nouwen.

Nouwen traveled extensively, mostly to the United States but also to France for an International L'Arche meeting. He gave numerous talks at churches and schools. He spoke to chaplains, teachers, and students. He spoke to bishops of the Anglican Diocese of Toronto; he led retreats for Baptist ministers, Catholic Workers, and a group from the Reorganized Latter Day Saints. The diversity of his outreach during this period is astonishing; he enjoyed visits from Korean evangelicals, and gave a seminar on sexuality for L'Arche Agape in Hull, Quebec. In addition, he continued his practice of spiritual-direction meetings with people in his community and beyond. Increasingly, the circle of this community grew and began to include people who would fly in from distant parts, including children's-TV-show personality Fred Rogers.

The year 1992 also marked the beginning of his fundraising work to help Daybreak build a spirituality center. He had long dreamed of living at such a place where he could lead retreats for Daybreak and the world. He officiated at numerous weddings, a funeral, a baptism, and a confirmation. He spoke to priests of Toronto as well as twice attended meetings of priests of L'Arche. He gave numerous talks. He spoke about Jesus at the Greenbelt Festival in England, on fundraising for the Marguerite Bourgeoys Family Service annual general meeting in Toronto, and on supporting people dealing with HIV "with special acknowledgment of their caregivers" in San

Francisco. He spoke to wealthy people attending a Ministry of Money retreat (a not-for-profit organization that assists wealthy people with philanthropic decision-making) and to artists at the Pacific School of Religion. He frequently spoke about the gift of L'Arche and community.

Even with such a packed work calendar, Nouwen still found time to relax and attend a performance of *Guys and Dolls* in New York City in September. It was also a time to cultivate friendships—more than a dozen friends visited him in 1992.

Nouwen gave only one retreat on the prodigal son in 1992. Perhaps it is understandable that he wasn't talking much about *The Return of the Prodigal Son* anymore. The parable and painting had consumed him since 1983. By 1992, nine years had passed since he first saw it, and Nouwen was in a different interior place. He had found the home and bonds of love he had been longing for. Nouwen's *need* for the painting had subsided.

The new theme that consumed him in 1992 was "being the beloved," as explored in his book *Life of the Beloved*, published the same year as *The Return of the Prodigal Son*. It is like a sister book to *Prodigal Son*, about what a person can experience once the primal needs for touch, home, and belonging are satisfied. When the search is not fearful and frantic, one can be still and truly hear the small voice that says, "You are the Beloved." This is the place where Nouwen had finally arrived: because of the painting, and the way Rembrandt transmuted his suffering to light; because of Nouwen's own breakdown and slow recovery by being held by his therapists in Winnipeg and his friends at Daybreak; because of his reconciliation with Ball; and because of the release of his resentment toward his father for not being able to give him the first love. Like all good icons, the painting had become an internalized image that had changed his inner landscape.

He spoke about the belovedness of all people with passion and zeal. At the Crystal Cathedral in California, Robert Schuller's congregation of the Reformed Church in America, he spoke to the 2,500 people in attendance as if he were addressing each one individually. "If you can hear just one thing I tell you let it be this: You are the beloved." He proclaimed everyone's belovedness with such conviction because he now felt it himself.

Other new themes began to emerge for Nouwen in 1992. Shortly after his birthday celebration, he gave a talk at the Christian Counselling Center in Toronto titled "Turn My Mourning into Dancing." It was the beginning of a period in which he wrote about the topic of death and dying. His own near-death experience in 1989, which he examined in *Beyond the Mirror: Reflections on Death and Life* (1990), laid the foundation for reflecting on this important theme.

Finally, Nouwen began writing about his new fascination with the trapeze troupe the Flying Rodleighs. During a month-long writing retreat with his friends Bart and Pat Gavigan in England, he explored the trapeze as a new metaphor for the spiritual life. As a metaphor, the trapeze act offered Nouwen some potent imagery— of risk, trust, and surrender. His icon, "his" prodigal son painting, slowly receded as the images of flyers and catchers began to fill his imagination. Notes from his retreat are titled "What Is the Risk?" He wondered if he could take his writing about the spiritual life in a whole new direction.

The Book and the 1990s Zeitgeist

Our intellect has achieved the most tremendous things but in the meantime, our spiritual dwelling has fallen into disrepair.
(C. G. Jung)[118]

Since its first release in 1992 *The Return of the Prodigal Son* has sold over one million copies. It is the book for which Henri Nouwen is most known. Yet, in May 1992, its publication barely registered. There were no critical accolades in the mainstream literary media. First-quarter sales were good, but this was likely based on Nouwen's name recognition for past works rather than social buzz. In retrospect, we can see that despite marginal publicity, readers bought the book because it spoke to their needs at that moment. In fact, it seemed to speak to the *zeitgeist* of a generation. What was happening in this period of American history to create such fertile conditions for the book's reception?

In 1992, as clerks in bookstores across North America were shelving *The Return of the Prodigal Son*, George H. W. Bush was serving his last year as president of the United States before the election of Bill Clinton in November 1992 and his inauguration in January 1993. Los Angeles descended into race riots following the acquittal of four Los Angeles Police Department officers for the beating of Rodney King. The USSR was dissolved; NAFTA, a historic trade agreement between the United States, Canada, and Mexico was signed; and, across the Atlantic in England, Prince Charles and Lady Diana separated. *Home Alone 2*, *Wayne's World*, *Reservoir Dogs*, and *Sister Act* were all popular films released in theaters. Nirvana, led by Kurt Cobain, was filling stadiums with "Smells Like Teen Spirit" from their album *Nevermind*. *The Jerry Springer Show*, *Law and Order*, *Star Trek: The Next Generation*, and *Married with Children* were being watched by millions of TV viewers. *The Oprah Winfrey Show* was in its seventh popular year, and grunge—flannel shirts, baby-doll dresses with army boots, and smudged eyeliner—was the fashion of the day. AIDS/HIV was still devastating lives, and, in a live broadcast, singer Sinéad O'Connor famously ripped a photograph of Pope John Paul II on *Saturday Night Live* in a protest against sexual abuse in the Catholic Church.

In the world of books, the *New York Times* bestseller list included such soon-to-be classics as Douglas Coupland's *Shampoo Planet*, Neil Gaiman's *Sandman* series, John Grisham's *Pelican Brief*, Toni Morrison's *Jazz*, and Terry MacMillan's *Waiting to Exhale*. Canadian Michael Ondaatje published *The English Patient* and won the Booker Prize.

At first glance, *The Return of the Prodigal Son* had little to add to this political and pop-cultural landscape. But the early 1990s was an era of earnest searching—personal, social, political—stemming in part from a shifting world order begun in the 1960s.

The decades that followed "the hippie movement" saw the rise of feminism, the men's movement, and ecological consciousness. Women were looking for liberation from a patriarchal system that stifled their autonomy and choices. Men, mirroring these voices for change, urged a reexamination of men's roles. A men's spirituality movement evolved that called for a deeper connection with self and God. The 1990s also marked the beginning of a growing sensitivity to the relationship between environmentalism and religion. *A Silent Spring*, published in 1962, the seminal work of Rachel Carson, an American marine biologist, had advanced a global environmental movement, and by the 1990s, theologians and others were making connections between their discipline and earth health. Creation spirituality, as articulated by Matthew Fox, also took root.[119]

Another important factor in the shifting world order can be traced back to the baby-boomer generation, who, as we noted earlier, responded to the loss of life and destruction of World War II and the Vietnam War by rejecting the value system of their parents' generation. They were looking for a different way of living. For many boomers (around 42 percent in the United States), organized religion had lost its place as a moral and ethical barometer. Rejecting the traditional church, they were looking for new sources of inspiration and guidance. The questions were still the same as those of earlier generations: Who am I? Why am I here? What is my purpose? How do I live? But the traditional responses didn't satisfy. People were looking for a spirituality that was both relevant to the new ways of living and powerful enough to provide a counterpoint to secular materialism. Many turned to books, and in 1992 they would have encountered two massive bestsellers: *The Celestine Prophecy: An Adventure* by James Redfield, and *A Return to Love: Reflections on the Principles of "A Course in Miracles"* by Marianne Williamson.

The Celestine Prophecy was published in 1993, but Redfield famously sold copies out of the trunk of his car for most of the year prior before finding a traditional publisher. The book was on the *New York Times* bestseller list for 165 weeks and for two years was the best-selling American book in the world. It was translated into thirty-five languages, and a film adaptation was released in 2000. "Why did this happen?" asks Redfield on his website, Celestine Vision. "I believe it happened because *The Celestine Prophecy* worked as clarification, in that the story represented a rise in the Spiritual consciousness many of us were pursuing at the very same time."[120]

Like *The Return of the Prodigal Son*, Redfield's book is told in a first-person narrative style. It is a recounting of the protagonist's spiritual awakening as he goes through a transitional period of his life. The main character must find and interpret a series of nine spiritual insights found in an ancient Peruvian manuscript. As in *The Return of the Prodigal Son*, there is a strong emphasis on the spiritual authority of the self to make choices. Additionally, both books follow a similar narrative arc wherein a hero sets out on a journey or spiritual quest, emerging from his ordeals with life-changing wisdom that he is now called to share with others.

Redfield, like Nouwen, uses various psychological concepts to support the essentially spiritual thrust of the book. Where it differs is Redfield's use of ancient Eastern traditions as the source for his insights. Here, Redfield was on trend. Globalism was very much afoot. The Soviet Union had collapsed and the Cold War was over. People were looking further afield for answers and taking other religions into account. The 1990s saw the publication of dozens of popular titles about Eastern religions for the Westerner. *A Path with Heart* by Jack Kornfield and *The Tibetan Book of Living and Dying* by Sogyal Rinpoche are two such examples.

Redfield also draws from New Age spirituality for his book. *New Age* is a term applied to a range of spiritual or religious beliefs and practices that gained momentum in the United States during the 1970s and 1980s. It tapped into the feeling, mentioned earlier, experienced among many boomers that traditional religion could no longer be trusted and that new sources of meaning were needed.

Marianne Williamson, a forty-year-old secular Jew from Texas, based her 1992 bestseller, *A Return to Love*, on one such new source. Her book was a distillation of *A Course in Miracles*, which had been published in 1976 and compiled by Helen Schucman and William Thetford. *A Course in Miracles* is described as "a curriculum for achieving spiritual transformation" that uses traditional Christian terminology but in very nontraditional ways. Williamson appeared on *The Oprah Winfrey Show* and with the power of that marketing boost, *A Return to Love* remained on the *New York Times* bestseller list for thirty-nine weeks, becoming the fifth-bestselling book in America that year.

Its similarity to Nouwen's *The Return of the Prodigal Son*, beginning with the word *return* in the title, is striking. Nouwen journeyed with a painting, Williamson with a book. She had first read *A Course in Miracles* in 1977, and by 1983, the same year that Nouwen saw the poster in Trosly, she was regularly lecturing on its teachings in Los Angeles and New York City. Both Nouwen and Williamson's books address fear, self-doubt, identity, and God's grace. Both contend that it is only by accepting God and by expressing love in our daily lives that we can find inner peace. Finally, both conclude that by following this path, not only will our own lives be more fulfilling, but we will also create a more peaceful and loving world for others.

A recurring theme in *A Return to Love*, as in *The Return of the Prodigal Son*, is how self-rejection affects our relationship with God. Nouwen writes that it is self-rejection that is our most common spiritual malaise, and he wants us to see that it is God who is seeking us while we are the ones doing the hiding. Williamson puts it this way:

> Our deepest fear is not that we are inadequate. Our deepest fear is that we are powerful beyond measure. It is our light, not our darkness that most frightens us. We ask ourselves, Who am I to be brilliant, gorgeous, talented, fabulous? Actually, who are you not to be? You are a child of God. Your playing small does not serve the world. There is nothing enlightened about shrinking so that other people won't feel insecure around you. We are all meant to shine, as children do. We were born to manifest the glory of God that is within us. It's

not just in some of us; it's in everyone. And as we let our own light shine, we unconsciously give other people permission to do the same. As we are liberated from our own fear, our presence automatically liberates others.[121]

The most pronounced difference between the books is the language. *A Return to Love* is based on Christian theology, but Williamson expresses herself in decidedly nontraditional, nonreligious ways. Nouwen's graceful use of language with its simple and clean pitch is part of its appeal, but he assumes familiarity and "buy in" on central tenets of the Christian faith. Another significant difference is Williamson's assertion that love can conquer all. Nouwen acknowledges that suffering will continue but that we can live it differently because of God's love.[122]

While *The Celestine Prophecy* and *A Return to Love* would have been hard to miss in the 1990s, other books were vying for reader's attention in the burgeoning self-help section of the local bookstore. Baby boomers were applying the same quest for peace in their inner lives that they had striven for on the world stage in their youth.

The self-help genre, with its blend of psychology and spirituality, had its beginning in 1936 with a book called *How to Win Friends and Influence People* by Dale Carnegie. It is one of the bestselling books of all time. Nouwen's generation took "self-help" to new levels. One contemporary, for instance, was M. Scott Peck, author of *The Road Less Traveled*, published in 1978; it spent 694 weeks, the equivalent of thirteen years, on the *New York Times* bestseller list.

Peck, born four years after Nouwen, was a psychiatrist, and his book focused on his core belief that "life is difficult," and that its problems can be only be addressed through self-discipline. His approach to self-discipline was infused not only with a general belief in the help of a higher power, which made his books particularly popular with twelve-step programs like Alcoholics Anonymous, but also with his specifically Christian personal beliefs.

Peck would reflect that readers were drawn to his book because he said things in it that they thought but didn't have the courage to say.[123] He covered such topics as dependency, taking responsibility, accepting suffering, and delaying gratification. A large portion of the book is dedicated to the psychology of love. He focuses particularly on romantic love: "While I generally find that great myths are great precisely because they represent and embody great universal truths ... the myth of romantic love is a dreadful lie. Perhaps it is a necessary lie in that it ensures the survival of the species by its encouragement and seeming validation of the falling-in-love experience that traps us into marriage. But as a psychiatrist I weep in my heart almost daily for the ghastly confusion and suffering that this myth fosters."[124]

Also reflecting the spirit of the times was *Love, Medicine and Miracles*, published in 1984 by Bernie Siegel. Siegel offers spiritual guidance on how to live with illness and mortality. Born a month after Nouwen, in October 1932, Siegel was a retired pediatric surgeon who believed that unconditional love was the most powerful stimulant of the immune system. He wrote, "The truth is: love heals. Miracles happen to exceptional patients every day—patients who have the courage to love."[125]

By 1992, the self-help genre was a full-blown industry. Many people were looking for books to improve their lives, especially in the area of career success. Two influential books that addressed this were Steven Covey's *Seven Habits of Highly Effective People* and *Awake the Giant Within* by entrepreneurial guru Anthony Robbins. These books have a slight tone of triumphalism, a feature foreign to *The Return of the Prodigal Son*—yet they are similar to *The Return of the Prodigal Son* in their focus on the psychology of change, or in Nouwen's language, transformation.

Stephen Richards Covey, like Bernie Siegel, was born just one month after Nouwen.[126] He was an American educator, author, and businessperson. Covey was also a Mormon, and *The Seven Habits* is considered by some to be a distillation of Mormon teachings. It was published in 1989 and sold twenty-five million copies worldwide. In 1992, US President Bill Clinton invited Covey to Camp David to counsel him on how to integrate the book into his presidency. In an interesting parallel, First Lady Hillary Clinton would later summon Nouwen to the White House as a spiritual advisor, based on her appreciation of *The Return of the Prodigal Son*.

While authors like Covey and Robbins were writing predominantly for people interested in the outward signs of success, Nouwen and others were aiming their books at people whose interests were more introspective. A common approach among these books, including *The Return of the Prodigal Son*, is the use of psychology to understand human nature.

The year 1992 is at the tail end of an era when Carl Jung's approach to healing eclipsed that of Freud. While Freud focused on dreams and the family social structure to help people, Jung used archetypes, fairy tales, myths, parables, and other folklore narratives to understand the human psyche. Jung was particularly focused on spiritual development. He felt people's spiritual lives were being overshadowed by the late nineteenth and twentieth centuries' preference for intellectual enlightenment. He wrote, "Our intellect has achieved the most tremendous things but in the meantime, our spiritual dwelling has fallen into disrepair."[127] Many writers steeped in the Jungian tradition, including Henri Nouwen, aimed to right the balance.

Jungian theory, especially the emphasis on the power of archetypes, fairy tales, myths, and parables to explore various psychological topics, was used to great effect by Joseph Campbell in his classic work *The Hero with a Thousand Faces*, published in 1949. *The Hero with a Thousand Faces* explores the archetypal hero that is universally shared by world mythologies. He called this universally shared myth the "monomyth." James Hillman, an American psychologist and scholar in Jungian thought, founded the field of archetypal psychology, which stresses the importance of imagination both in the experience of psyche and in life itself.

In the year that Nouwen's *The Return of the Prodigal Son* was published, another book appeared that followed in the path of Campbell and Hillman: *Care of the Soul: A Guide for Cultivating Depth and Sacredness in Everyday Life* by Thomas Moore. Moore, an American psychotherapist, spent twelve years studying to become a Roman Catholic priest before changing his mind just before ordination. Moore draws from theories of Jung, Freud, Plato, and others to reexamine Western archetypes and myths, citing Demeter and Persephone, Narcissus and Odysseus, as well as Jesus, as models of personal growth and transformation. The premise of his book is that our souls need to be cared for differently from the way we attend to our bodies or minds. "The great malady of the 20th century," he writes, "implicated in all of our troubles and affecting us individually and socially is 'loss of soul.' When soul is neglected, it doesn't just go away; it appears symptomatically in obsessions, addictions, violence and loss of meaning."[128] Moore, calling to mind *The Return of the Prodigal Son*, draws on his own life for examples and urges readers to go deeper into feelings they are often ashamed of. "Remember," he writes, "soul appears most easily in those places where we feel more inferior."[129] Moore's book became an instant bestseller and spent forty-six weeks on the *New York Times* bestseller list. One reviewer remarked, "*Care of the Soul* has struck a national nerve."[130]

Moore's *Care of the Soul* offered a philosophy for living that involved accepting our humanity rather than struggling to transcend it. The book is so packed with resonant themes in *The Return of the Prodigal Son* that it is not surprising that Nouwen was asked to write a promotional piece for the back cover of the first edition.[131]

Also from 1992, using archetypes and myth, was the bestseller *Women Who Run with the Wolves: Myths and Stories of the Wild Woman Archetype* by Jungian analyst and poet Clarissa Pinkola Estés. It spent nearly half a year on the *New York Times* bestseller list over a three-year span, a record at the time. It is a feminist retelling of Campbell's monomyth. Using myths and stories, Estés helps women embark on a quest for warmth, love, and support. It calls for transformation and release from stories that have kept women in submission.

Again, it has a similarity to Nouwen's book: use of story, focus on the importance of dying to the old self, and spiritual maturity. Estés tells readers that "to love is to stay with." She continues: "It means to emerge from a fantasy world into a world where sustainable love is possible, face to face, bones to bones, a love of devotion. To love means to stay when every cell says 'run!'"[132]

While feminist readers were buying titles like *Women Who Run with the Wolves* and other seminal books from the time,[133] men had their own books to choose from. *Iron John: A Book About Men* by Robert Bly came out in 1990 and instantly became the voice of a generation of men looking for direction on how to live their masculinity. A popular American poet, Bly used Jungian psychology to analyze the Grimms' fairy tale "Iron John," about a boy maturing into adulthood. Bly believed that this story contained lessons from the past that were of great importance to modern men. He presented a masculinity that was vigorous, protective, and emotionally centered.

Nouwen was part of this generation (in fact, he joined a men's group at L'Arche Daybreak[134] inspired by *Iron John*), as was Richard Rohr, a Franciscan priest, who published *The Wild Man's Journey: Reflections on Male Spirituality* (1992; coauthored with John Martos).

Like *Iron John*, Rohr and Martos's book uses myths and fairy tales to explore masculine identity, but this time within a Christian context.

Rohr and Nouwen weren't the only Christian authors contributing to the publishing trend of using folklore to convey spiritual truths. Eugene Peterson, a Presbyterian minister best known for his recasting of the Bible as *The Message*, published in 1992 his book *Under the Unpredictable Plant: An Exploration of Vocational Holiness*.[135] It had a lot in common with Nouwen's earlier books *The Wounded Healer* and *Creative Ministry* in that it identified a propensity among American clergy to approach ministry as "religious careerism" along the capitalist business model. Peterson's book was also like *The Return of the Prodigal Son* in the way that Peterson used a story from the Bible to probe the spiritual dimension of the pastoral calling. In his case, he used the book of Jonah as a structural narrative. He saw the story as a subversive illustration of how to be an ideal minister. He then built on this with other metaphors and stories to help ministers clarify their vocation and live it out. Peterson believed, in an echo from Nouwen's approach to art, that stories need to be "entered" into to be understood and activate meaning in our lives.[136] The similarities between Peterson and Nouwen merit further exploration.

A final theme that Nouwen's book tapped into was the search by readers for books that helped them grow up. Baby boomers were just entering their thirties and forties in the 1990s and, having rejected their parents as role models, needed new ways of entering into this phase of life. American psychologist David Richo wrote a book to respond to this need. *How to Be an Adult: A Handbook in Psychological and Spiritual Integration* (1991) incorporated all the approaches and trends of the day: developmental psychology, Eastern traditions, personal transformation, and Christian spirituality. And like Nouwen in *The Return of the Prodigal Son* and other authors we have looked at, Richo uses the metaphor of the heroic journey—departure, struggle, and return—to show readers the way to psychological and spiritual maturity. In the introduction, Richo writes, "In this book we explore departure and struggle by working through the drama of childhood, by assertiveness (asking for what we want, being clear and taking responsibility for our own feelings), by dealing with fear, anger and guilt, by building self-esteem, by maintaining personal boundaries, by achieving true intimacy, by integrating ourselves flexibly, and by befriending our Shadow."[137]

Final Thoughts

The Return of the Prodigal Son shares many characteristics of the publishing *zeitgeist* of the early 1990s. Nouwen's book marries the psychological with the spiritual; it utilizes parables and stories, particularly the hero journey; and it addresses a generation's concerns for coping with life's big questions. Themes such as how to love others and self, how to live loss, and how to mature into adulthood are very much part of that trend.

But, as much as it tapped into popular themes, *The Return of the Prodigal Son* was not a runaway bestseller when it first appeared. Books written by Christians with overt Christian language were not as popular as books that spoke a more psychological, spiritual-but-not-religious language.

In some ways, *The Return of the Prodigal Son* was for people who had read the other books and were still hurting, confused, and/or searching for peace. There are no promises of quick fixes or permanent change in Nouwen's work. There is no need to conquer or master ourselves in *The Return of the Prodigal Son*. It is more a matter of changing our perception of our imperfections and wounds. Like Elijah, who heard the voice of God in the stillness and quiet of the desert, Nouwen doesn't proclaim. He encourages, suggests, invites. This may contribute to the book's relative hiddenness in the cultural mainstream. By using his own experience, Nouwen shows us that the gift is often *in* the struggle and that, by claiming our woundedness, we are more able to love ourselves as God loves us. The cultural norm is to strive to be spectacular, the winner, the best; but Nouwen's voice is more countercultural.

He invites us to consider an alternate way. Nouwen was fond of telling a story of the two voices. He said that for most of his life he had heard two voices in his head. The first one encouraged him to be popular, relevant, and successful, and above all to make a mark on the world. The second one said, "Keep Jesus as the centre." We see this internal struggle play out in *The Return of the Prodigal Son*. Nouwen becomes the "hero" because he uses courage and maturity to choose the downward way. The way of the unspectacular. The way of love. His message isn't about winning. It is about loving others and claiming our maternal and paternal energies for the good of all.

Another important difference is that while Nouwen is the "protagonist" of his book, the real subject of the story is God. *The Return of the Prodigal Son* is a portrait, not only of himself, but also of God. Nouwen uses his deep understanding of the psychological makeup of humans; the purpose, however, is not to reveal *us*, but to reveal the divine.

The Return of the Prodigal Son ends on an ambiguous note. Nouwen has claimed his fatherhood, but he never suggests that he has it all together. Instead, he simply offers us a way to rethink our way to spiritual maturity. He calls it a "dreadful" choice but one that has to be taken. The book ends with a challenge—one that is not "me" focused but "other" focused. Will we claim our belovedness and from there claim our likeness to God? Will we become generative, nurturing, and loving? Will we bless and give life? These are the questions we are left to ponder as the book draws to a close.

Chapter 4 ⁓
Response to
The Return of the Prodigal Son

I am confident that this book is my best book and that it can speak deeply to people at this time. The letters and phone calls that I receive are too convincing to doubt that.
—Henri Nouwen[138]

Nouwen was very pleased with *The Return of the Prodigal Son*. A month after publication, in a letter to Ed Wojcicki, a longtime correspondent and journalist, Nouwen wrote,

> I am really grateful to you for your warm words about *The Return of the Prodigal Son*. It is a very important book for me and I feel that I put myself more into that book than into any other. You would do me a great favour if you would recommend it to friends who may be able to profit from this book. I am very proud of this book and I hope it can connect me in a good way with many people in their journeys.[139]

He was even more effusive with his editor Bill Barry: "I am confident that this book is my best book and that it can speak deeply to people at this time. The letters and phone calls that I receive are too convincing to doubt that."[140] Indeed, the book was getting a very warm and excited response from readers. Nouwen received more letters for this book than any other. "While the other books published by Doubleday were well received," Nouwen writes, "I have never received such intense, personal, deeply moving responses."

Yet, in spite of such a swell of reader response, sales were slowing. Nouwen wondered if it had to do with the high price of the book (it sold for $25; $45 in today's money) as well as its "particular style." He also suspected that poor marketing by Doubleday was part of the problem. He urged his publisher to do more to drive sales, again citing L'Engle's book in the *New York Times*. He wrote,

> I also wonder whether you would be willing to advertise the book in a few major magazines. I saw a very powerful advertisement for Madeleine L'Engle in the last issue of the New York Times book review section. I know Madeleine and I feel that the kind of things that we both write about are on the same wave length. I really believe that one or two big ads in major newspapers would give the "Prodigal son" book a significant push.[141]

Another thought was to reprint the book as a paperback with a better price point. A new subtitle was suggested to appeal to more readers. Nouwen liked this change, and the paperback edition came out as *The Return of the Prodigal Son: A Story of a Homecoming* in July 1993.

Nouwen was disappointed in the diminished quality of the illustrations of this new edition, however. He was still adamant that the reader have a full image of Rembrandt's painting to look at while reading. But the need to bring costs down meant fewer and poorer-quality plates. In a letter to Lydia Banducci, Nouwen's publishing assistant at the time, Barry would write, "It is no idle compliment to Nouwen that the power of the book is in the meditation, and what appeal the book may lose because of the reduced number of illustrations is more than compensated by the many more readers who will come to experience the work at a more attractive price."[142]

While it didn't get national coverage, as Nouwen hoped, it did get the attention of Fernand Bonneure, a Belgian prose writer, poet, and publisher, who wrote a long review in *The Dutch Review of Books* (*De Nederlandse Boekengids*) in January 1992. Bonneure called it an "excellent meditation book." Other reviews in Holland and Germany were equally complimentary.

In the United States, the book received little critical attention. Between 1992 and 1994 there were fewer than a dozen reviews, mostly in small, local papers. While every mention of the book was positive, it was getting lost among books with bigger profiles. The largest publication to review the book was the *New Oxford Review*, a conservative Catholic magazine with a circulation of twelve thousand. Luis R. Gamez, a regular contributor to the magazine, wrote: "A beautiful book, as beautiful in the simple clarity of its wisdom as in the terrible beauty of the transformation to which it calls us."[143]

While other books were winning awards and stacking up the reviews, the most high-profile acknowledgment received by *The Return of the Prodigal Son* came in winning first runner-up in the New Zealand chapter of the Christian Booksellers Association in 1995. In fact, the book, notwithstanding steady sales, was so low-profile that by 1999, it was considered a "hidden treasure" by Michael Leach, an editor and publisher who had worked in the past with Nouwen at Crossroad Publishing. In "Hidden Treasures: The 10 Best Spiritual Books You've Never Read," Leach speculated on books that might one day become classics. "We used to think of a classic as a book that lasted a hundred years. Today, with more than 50,000 new titles published every year, the average shelf life of a book is shorter than this year's NBA season. A classic is 10 years. Are there any spiritual books published in the last couple of years that we can expect to see on the shelves 10 years from now?" *The Return of the Prodigal Son* made the list.[144]

It was not the critics selling *The Return of the Prodigal Son*; it was readers. The book had an underground buzz—with readers finding and buying it for each other. The reasons for the popularity of the book among readers are revealed through the letters they wrote to Nouwen.

Reader Response

Almost every letter begins with a thank-you. Readers were grateful that Nouwen had had the courage to be so vulnerable with his weaknesses. Carol wrote, "I admire your decision to enter into the parable yourself in the writing. This is what makes the book so healing. You are in effect laying down your life."[145]

Adele from Montreal echoed this idea:

> I am writing to you after having read *The Return of the Prodigal Son*. I was profoundly touched by your immense courage to reveal your weakness. Not many people are capable of this. To be able to express yourself so profoundly and yet so simply is a true gift, and it moved me very much. You taught me a wonderful lesson of humility. Without knowing you, you lit the way to God for me. I still have a long journey ahead, but as you say so well in your book, I do not have to follow the path alone. Thank you for the beautiful words you have written, please continue to light up people's lives.

This idea that Nouwen "lit the way to God" is a common refrain in the letters. Jeff wrote,

> The Prodigal obviously pained you in the writing; I'm deeply grateful for the pain. The book resounds in me with chords

long ungrounded, you suggest a key to home. . . . Henri, your book on Rembrandt's Prodigal astonishes me, not as an intellectual game but as a gift of life; I am deeply grateful to you for working it through and sharing it with us. I'm not home yet, but it points a way. At least I see where I have been for decades and where I need to go.

The book inspired people. A diocesan priest from Manila, Philippines, wrote, "Father it is not only your works that touch and inspire me but also your very life."

It struck a chord with readers who had turned away from God and felt ashamed to return. A particularly moving letter came from a prisoner in Ghana. Joseph was a married man and father who was serving a fourteen-year sentence for forging accounts. He had spent the first seven years in solitary confinement. He read *The Return of the Prodigal Son*, and it changed how he viewed his life:

As a prisoner I very much consider myself as somebody who has "wandered from the Father." At this moment I have repented of all my youthful excesses, and pray sincerely that I may be truly guided into my spiritual home. Thanks from the very depths of my heart for giving me greater spiritual insights. You are really a spiritual master and I also thank God that he has endowed you with such noble gifts which has enabled you to console the marginal in society and even sending me rays of hope and comfort in my Tamale prison.

Barry, a professor in an American Christian arts college, confessed to having an affair while married and committing other "deliberate sins." He thanked Nouwen for beginning the process of opening his heart to God: "This may sound strange, but as the words penetrated my soul I would have to stop and talk to this wonderful God whom I had known for years but had not really wanted to approach because of fear. Paragraph one on p. 121 describes me quite precisely—much theological training, a deep desire for closeness with God but a strange sense of fear, the paralyzing kind that you correctly label one of the great human tragedies."

Nouwen's book helped readers who struggled with feelings of unworthiness to be received back by God after turning away. Denise, a middle-aged woman from Maryland, articulated a feeling familiar to so many readers:

> I have come to understand that for most of my life I have denied myself the dream that I could be "at home," not feeling that I really deserved one. . . . I have been pushed, forced to see that God does love me. As you express so well in the book. And this has been the greatest gift. At the same time, it is also intimidating and fearful because the past does not want to "let go" so easily. I have come to know that my whole life, whenever I have been gifted by grace or had some success, I have undercut my happiness in another way. I think I was punishing myself first, so God wouldn't. It took me a long time to come to grips with just how unworthy I felt. In passing through my own tears of grief I have confronted this devil of unworthiness and begun to overcome her.

Other letters contain stories of how the book transformed lives. In at least two cases, it saved marriages. Marie wrote that *The Return of the Prodigal Son* had "quickened her husband's life." With her husband's heart opened again he was more available to their relationship. "God bless you," she continues. "May He keep you writing and cracking open stone cold hearts."

A teacher shared a similar story. She had been using Nouwen's book in class, and it had a profound effect on one of her adult students:

This term while using your book, one of the medical doctors had a daughter whom he refused to talk with for several years because of a marriage he didn't approve of. His anger and resentment was destroying his marriage, hurting his other children and eating away at him. Through the course of reading this book, he and I had lunch together many times, and he began to cry and share his inner fears of being hurt again by his daughter if he welcomed her home, and his grief over a daughter who had accidentally died (age 2½ years old) while he and his wife were medical missionaries in Africa. As he began to hear again about God's unconditional love, he reunited with his daughter, allowed the grief for his other daughter to surface and be dealt with.

Other parents wrote about the experience of alienation from their children. They spoke of how Nouwen's book made them live the waiting in a different way. One mother whose son had cut off ties with the family wrote, "I read a little; cried a lot." A father whose schizophrenic son, Embert, had been missing for ten years wrote in an article inspired by the book, "Often I ask myself how I would react should Embert return. Would I be able to welcome him like the forgiving father in the biblical parable and the Rembrandt painting? I hope and pray I would have enough love to do as the compassionate father did. I am strengthened in this hope by Nouwen's moving book and by having seen Rembrandt's powerful painting."[146]

Other readers inspired by the book spoke of it changing the path of their lives. Matthew wrote, "Your book has proved to be a turning point in my life. I am now seeking discernment as to whether I have a monastic vocation."

Many readers shared which of the sons from the parable they related to (more elder sons than younger sons), and all reported a better self-awareness and self-knowledge. "Your book is a grace!" one woman, a nun, exclaimed.

The book was also well received by young-adult readers. A bundle of letters from university students who had read the book in their literature classes revealed that the book meant different things depending on the age of the reader. One student wrote, "I feel rechristianized!" Another, "It was comforting, reassuring, exciting, turbulent and depressing all at the same time." One letter, from John, shared how the book helped him reestablish a relationship with his father:

> On Monday evening, I got into a fight with my father. He was upset that I never call or come home, he felt like I didn't care about my family. My father's father never did anything with my father and was almost neglectful toward him. Therefore, my father goes out of his way to show his love for me. He has made it his life to show that he cares for me. When I left the house for college, I wanted to get away from my family. I have had a lot of fun and many other responsibilities that have kept me from keeping in touch with my family. That is what this fight was about. When I was reading all of the questions going through the younger son's head . . . I could really relate to him. At the same time I felt awful because I had basically disowned my family as he did by asking for his inheritance early. I called my father back on Wednesday night while I was in the middle of the book and when he answered he asked if this was the prodigal son. It was really ironic and strange. He and I are going for dinner on Friday, and I hope he is waiting for me with open arms because I need him back in my life.

For many readers, the book leads to a reckoning with their identity as mother or father. One single woman confided that she had given up a son for adoption. After reading *The Return of the Prodigal Son*, she was reclaiming her motherhood (the pregnancy, the birth, the time she had with her son before adoption) even if she was not actively mothering her son. She explained that she was even waiting for him differently now that she had read the book. She hoped he would reach out to her, and she was getting herself ready to be a welcoming mother when he did.

A nun with the Little Sisters of Jesus, Charles de Foucauld, in Montreal asked for Nouwen's prayers that she "may learn to be more maternal."

Perhaps one of the most beautiful exchanges took place between Nouwen and an architect, who wrote to thank him for the book and to share pain he was experiencing around being rejected by a younger colleague. The colleague had left the firm with a girlfriend without a forwarding address. The architect was heartbroken. He wrote,

> Some months ago I purchased "The Return of the Prodigal Son" but for some strange reason put it in a stack of books on my bedside table with something of dread in my heart at starting it. . . . Two nights ago I picked [it] up . . . took a deep breath and said, "Well, here goes." . . . Your essays on the father hit me pretty hard. Am I blind to the ways of the world? Am I too judgmental? Am I too hard on this "younger son and younger daughter"? I must tell you that they are in my prayers both morning and night, and I would go running down the road to greet them if I knew they were coming, my arms outstretched and my tired hands ready to hug both of them.

The letter caught up with Nouwen in Europe, where he was on sabbatical. He wrote back immediately:

I am truly grateful that you took the time and energy to let me know what the book meant to you.

As you will have noticed, this book could never have been written if I had not been part of a community of mentally handicapped people. Although life in that community is not always easy, it continues to be for me a great source of energy and vision.

I deeply appreciate your sharing with me [your] story. . . . Meanwhile I am still struggling to become the father as Jesus portrays him in the parable. I frankly think that we will never be the perfect fathers we would like to be, but simply knowing that we are called to not only a new childhood but a new fatherhood can give us a way to live our life gratefully.[147]

While the general tone of letters was one of gratitude, in rare instances, they included criticism. However, this was usually delivered with a gentle touch. One criticism repeated by several readers is the lack of insight into the female perspective. Janet, a doctor, wondered about sibling rivalry between the brothers and what she sees as their sister lurking in the shadows. She suggests there is an important interplay between the genders and imagines the thoughts of the siblings: "How come she gets to have it so easy while we men work? Do you love her more? And the prodigal Eve says: Why do I have to be so distant and estranged from you men? Can't I come home and become part of what you're doing?"

Another woman, Donna, wrote to Nouwen about the shadow woman in the painting:

For some reason I assumed that all the figures in the painting would be discussed in the book. I was looking forward to a chapter on what I refer to as the "shadows" that are evident in the picture. I was very impressed that Rembrandt placed a woman at the scene of the reunion. Of course, the Mother! . . .

If you ever update the book I wish you would consider addressing the mother and other shadows.

Donna was also offended by Nouwen's use of the word "selfless," saying that she has seen it used to justify the acceptance of abuse and lack of respect. "The word selfless to me connotes a perversion of love that turns a person into a doormat. It caused people to remain in relationships that rob them of their dignity and self-respect. It literally means not having a self or forgetting who you are." Interestingly, this is a theme that is more active than ever, in the present twenty-first century, in part due to the impact of the MeToo movement.

The gender imbalance didn't affect everyone, however. Jolene wrote, "Usually I am quite conscious of gender sensitive language, but although I am a woman I visualize myself as the Father, sons and siblings from Rembrandt's painting. I became aware of this 2/3 of the way through the book when I recommended it to a woman friend and realized the feminine gender is not mentioned."

While some readers questioned the lack of attention to the female perspective, another felt that the book celebrated the breaking of the spirit of the younger son, turning him "flaccid." The writer, Alistair, was a former student of Nouwen's and was coming to the book as a therapist and non-Christian. He had concerns with the way the younger son "has been tamed": "For me in the painting the trickster, the youthful, spirited, passionate, sexual, adventurous son is reduced to rags . . . and I think that all too often in my own life, the same is true. My desire to 'do the right thing' smothers the fun-loving, sometimes irreverent, irascible side of me." Alistair admitted that much of his reaction was tied to the church. "The Church stifles life!" he wrote. Alistair saw the dilemma as an archetypal dynamic between the *puer*, "the eternal boy," and *senex*, "the Old Man." "They don't need forgiveness," he wrote.

This letter is insightful because it brings up two competing aspects of Nouwen's personality. *The Return of the Prodigal Son* addresses them but only obliquely. The first is that Nouwen can be seen as the *puer aeternus*. Michael O'Laughlin was the first to make the observation in his biography *God's Beloved: A Spiritual Biography of Henri Nouwen*, and subsequent writers have repeated the insight. Nouwen had a side of him that could be childlike.[148] But Nouwen was also the elder calling for containment. While not as present in *The Return of the Prodigal Son*, in "Returning," his 1988 retreat on the prodigal son, Nouwen focuses more directly on this theme, particularly as it relates to the body and incarnation. He says,

> Both sons have no way of celebrating the body. The younger son is about dissipation. The older son is about slaving. . . . The parable story helps us reclaim the body as a temple, as a good place. We let it be loved and cared for, touched. We are incarnate. We can enjoy our createdness. Some spirituality has become disincarnate. But we are called to bring the body home and bring spirit home with it. No guilt! No punishment! We feel shame but God says it is okay. Gradually, you discover that you are keeping more things hidden than you know. In light of God's forgiveness you find more of what you have hidden.[149]

Nouwen's interpretation of the parable as Rembrandt painted it supports the idea of God encouraging his children to live in freedom. In Nouwen and Rembrandt's understanding, it is as though God says, "Go, son. Go, daughter. It is good. Take a risk. When you come back I will be here for you." Returning, as Nouwen says, is a movement that involves a leaving—both are encouraged and welcomed by the loving Father. Far from restricting us, God gives us the freedom to explore our lives with creativity and self-expression.

In addition to the hundreds of letters from general readers, the book also drew the attention of some prominent people. Vincente Fox, the former president of Mexico, brought it with him on a state visit to China.[150] Pope Francis puts it on his top-ten list of books that have influenced him.[151] Hillary Rodham Clinton, however, might have been Nouwen's most famous and vocal reader. In a letter to Sue Mosteller, she wrote, "I have given *The Return of the Prodigal Son* to many people, including heads of state. It inspires me still and I thank you for continuing to spread Henri Nouwen's message of love and joy."[152] Clinton first read the book in 1994. In an interview with the *Washington Post*, she remarked that one passage in particular struck her:

> The phrase is, "the discipline of gratitude." . . . I don't mean to sound out of touch, but there's so much that goes on in my life on a daily basis that I'm grateful for despite everything else that's going on. And then to think about gratitude as a discipline so that every day gives you an opportunity to practice that gratitude, is very important to me. So there are days when I'm more chipper than others, but there isn't a day when I'm not trying at least to remember and be grateful for all that I have.[153]

Clinton was so impressed with the book that in 1994 she had her assistant write to Nouwen to see if they could meet. Nouwen's sabbatical and then unexpected death in 1996 prevented the meeting from taking place, but Clinton's admiration for the book didn't end with his death. In 2000, she picked it as her favorite book for *O, The Oprah Magazine*, saying,

> Nouwen's book contains universal, timeless lessons for people of all religions, backgrounds and cultures. It really is

about how our heavenly Father, God, loves us despite our shortcomings and failings. For me it was a call to the discipline of gratitude and forgiveness. And I certainly have had plenty of occasions to use both. I would encourage everyone to read it, particularly if they are going through difficult times in their lives.[154]

Again, in her memoir, *What Happened*, about the 2016 American presidential election, Hillary Clinton mentioned nineteen books that helped her cope after the campaign—and one of them was *The Return of the Prodigal Son*, a book she says she continues to return to in hard times.[155]

Ongoing Impact

While the book got off to a slow start when it was first published, it has since become Nouwen's bestseller. An internet search on any given day will turn up hundreds of references to the book, especially news of upcoming retreats, workshops, lectures, and book clubs centered on the book.

In 1999, it may have been considered a "hidden treasure," but by 2011 it was cited in *25 Books Every Christian Should Read: A Guide to Essential Spiritual Classics*. Editor Julia L. Roller polled leaders and thinkers in the field of Christian spirituality about what books they considered classics. Nouwen's *The Return of the Prodigal Son* is number 25 after *Mere Christianity* by C. S. Lewis and *The Seven Storey Mountain* by Thomas Merton and twenty-two other titles. In the *25 Books* volume, Richard Rohr describes *The Return of the Prodigal Son* as "a masterpiece of good theology that is applied to the healing of relationships in a way that really touches people."[156]

The same year, *The Return of the Prodigal Son* was named "the most beautiful book of all time" by *Trouw*, a newspaper in the

Netherlands. *Trouw* is the sixth-most-circulated national daily in the Netherlands, reaching nearly 100,000 readers.[157] Cultural theologian Frank Bosman of Tilburg University said of the award, "It is something like proclaiming Mother Teresa to be the holiest person on earth. No one can be against it."

Maria ter Steeg, Nouwen's good friend and also a translator of a number of his books, remarked, "It is perhaps his best work, it has a good structure and when you read it you can see that his soul is in it." There are other indicators of the ongoing impact and influence of *The Return of the Prodigal Son*. One is the number of other artistic works it inspires. Nouwen received many of these in the mail: poems, photographs of sculptures, and songs. More recently, Theo Lens, a Dutch musician, has created a concept album based on *The Return of the Prodigal Son*.[158] At least three musicals have been inspired by the book—one in Brazil and two in the Netherlands.[159] Another measure is how often the book is cited by other spiritual writers—more than any of book of his. Tara Brach, for example, an American teacher in the Buddhist tradition, gave a talk based on *The Return of the Prodigal Son*, calling it a book that she finds "deep" and "layered with meaning" with much to offer the Buddhist practitioner.

Chapter 5 ～∽
Living the Painting

It now has been more than six years since I first saw the Rembrandt poster at Trosly and five years since I decided to make L'Arche my home. As I reflect on these years, I realize that the people with a mental handicap and their assistants made me "live" Rembrandt's painting more completely than I could have anticipated.

—Henri Nouwen[160]

When *The Return of the Prodigal Son* begins, Nouwen pitches his story as a spiritual adventure. He's the protagonist, the hero on a journey. He's our *anam cara*, our soul friend, our wise guide. He is our witness to God in the world.

When the book ends, Nouwen comes to a surprising conclusion. For much of the adventure Nouwen was following God's call to return home and to let the internalized younger and elder son receive God's welcoming love. But as he got closer to home, he realized there was a greater call beyond the call to return. It was the call to become the father who welcomes *others* home and calls for a celebration. Nouwen is "awed by this call" (*Prodigal Son*, 110). Our hero, our guide, goes out ahead of us to explore the territory of returning home to the Father and comes back with the challenge of claiming spiritual adulthood. The book ends as he sets out on this final passage. How does he fare? Was he able to give up childhood? Was he able to sustain the "dreadful emptiness"?

First, let's review the adventure to which we have been witness.

Nouwen's Spiritual Adventure: A Review

Nouwen's story begins with this provocative sentence: "A seemingly insignificant encounter with a poster presenting a detail of Rembrandt's *The Return of the Prodigal Son* set in motion a long spiritual adventure that brought me to a new understanding of my vocation and offered me new strength to live it" (*Prodigal Son*, 3).

He explains that at the time of this encounter he was "dead tired." He was "anxious, lonely, restless, and very needy" after a "long self-exposing journey" (*Prodigal Son*, 4). One day, he saw the poster and was drawn to the intimacy between the two figures. His eyes absorbed "the warm red of the man's cloak, the golden yellow of the boy's tunic, and the mysterious light engulfing them both" (*Prodigal Son*, 4). Above all, he was drawn to the man's hands on the shoulders of the boy. In that moment, "The son-come-home was all I was and that I wanted to be" (*Prodigal Son*, 4).

But in the beginning, he was not the boy. He was the bystander. He was *watching* the beautiful reunion between loving father and exhausted son at a wistful distance. His initiation into stepping into the role of prodigal son only happens later—after years of living at L'Arche Daybreak. There among the people with handicaps and their assistants, he sensed safety and belonging and dared to place himself at the Father's feet. It meant giving up a sense of control, and he was resistant: "These years at Daybreak have not been easy. . . . I really did not have an inkling of how difficult the journey would be. I did not realize how deeply rooted my resistance was and how agonizing it would be to 'come to my senses', fall on my knees, and let my tears flow freely. I did not realize how hard it would be to become truly part of the great event that Rembrandt's painting portrays" (*Prodigal Son*, 13).

The Great Event

What is this great event for Nouwen? It is the meeting of humanity with divine love. It is human longing meeting its source and satisfaction. As we noted earlier, before seeing the poster, Nouwen had been writing and speaking about the difference between God's love and human love. He called God's love "first love" and the love between people as "second love." First love was about "God's kiss," as Plato named it, or as the "primal intimacy" as we have seen that John O'Donohue understood it. It is the perfect love, the original love, set in our hearts long before we are born. Second love is human love, which is only a refraction of the first. Nouwen understood that much human suffering comes from expecting from the second love what only the first love can give.

One of the reasons the poster hit Nouwen with such force was that he suddenly had an image for this first love. He saw Rembrandt's portrayal of the embrace, and it "imprinted on his soul." He says, "It brought me in touch with the ongoing yearning of the human spirit, the yearning for a final return, an unambiguous sense of safety, a lasting home" (*Prodigal Son*, 5).

The great event is also linked to a vastly different God than we might expect:

Looking at the way in which Rembrandt portrays the father, there came to me a whole new interior understanding of tenderness, mercy, and forgiveness. Seldom, if ever, has God's immense compassionate love been expressed in such a poignant way. Every detail of the father's figure—his facial expression, his posture, the color of his dress, and most of all, the still gesture of his hands—speaks of the divine love for humanity that existed from the beginning and ever will be (*Prodigal Son*, 88).

Seeing this great event portrayed by Rembrandt was not abstract for Nouwen. It was a lived experience that would take years to unfold and many more to manifest. Again, Daybreak was the crucible of transformation. When he saw the poster for the first time he was the bystander. Then, after the welcome and celebration of the community, he allowed himself to enter the painting as the kneeling prodigal son. But life in community sharpened his awareness of his shadow side—he was also the resentful elder son. Living with people with handicaps revealed to Nouwen his own (see *Prodigal Son*, 127).

This journey was both an external and internal one. Externally, he would have to leave Daybreak to heal from depression; internally, he was led to an inner place he hadn't been before.

We, as readers, are witness to many radical calls brought about by the painting. This is the first: Nouwen is called to claim his sonship and his identity as the child of God. He is no longer the bystander looking at the main event with distant curiosity and suppressed longing. He moves to the center of the painting. He acknowledges that he is both the prodigal son and the elder son, the one who runs away and the one who stays but has emotional distance. He is the son of a loving parent who welcomes the children home.

But there is more. Nouwen's encounter with Rembrandt's painting initiates another challenge: to claim spiritual fatherhood. Everything in Nouwen resists. Can he give up the security of childhood? He knows it will not be easy and that he will need a lot of support. Yet he accepts this personal and vocational challenge. He says, "I must trust that I am capable of becoming the Father I am called to be" (*Prodigal Son*, 120).

Four years after publishing this proclamation, Nouwen was dead. How did he live those final years becoming the father?

Nouwen's Commitment and Leadership at Daybreak

One way to get a sense of Nouwen at Daybreak after the publication of *The Return of the Prodigal Son* is to listen to the stories of people who lived with him. One such story comes from *Befriending Life*, a collection of essays about Nouwen edited by Beth Porter. Mary Bastedo, a contributor to the book and a long-term assistant at Daybreak, writes that she observed a transformation in Nouwen and the community. Her perspective is especially helpful because she met Nouwen when he first arrived in 1986, and then spent several years away from Daybreak, returning in the summer of 1993, just in the period after the publication of *The Return of the Prodigal Son*. Here are some of her observations:

> In June 1993 when I returned to Daybreak, I found that both Nouwen and the community had been through a transformation. Nathan Ball had become the community leader. The shared vision and good relationship that had emerged between Nouwen and Ball brought stability. It was the first time responsibility for Daybreak's spiritual life had been separated from the role of community leader.
>
> The farm manager's bungalow had become a retreat house, where both Nouwen and Sue Mosteller lived, with a new wheelchair-accessible chapel in the basement. There

was a well-attended daily Eucharist at 8:30 a.m. Once a week it was an Anglican Eucharist, celebrated by Wendy Lywood, an Anglican priest who had come to live in one of the community houses. A new ecumenical harmony had emerged. Non-Catholics were feeling at home. A liturgical dance troupe had been formed. Nouwen had established a pastoral team of 15 assistants and core members. He had taught some core members to be altar servers. Some assistants had been mandated to give reflections on the Word, having taken a workshop with Nouwen. Traditions were developing for Holy Week, always involving the core members in ways that enriched the liturgies.[161]

Bastedo also observed that because of Nouwen's leadership, more baptisms were happening involving people with no previous religious affiliations; pastoral visits were coordinated to community members who were ill; and a bat mitzvah for a Jewish core member led to deeper embrace of its interfaith reality.

The transformation of Daybreak's community life paralleled a personal transformation in Nouwen. Bastedo wrote, "He had grown in inner peace. When I walked in the chapel in 1993, I knew he had found his place at Daybreak. He was much more secure, comfortable, more fatherly. He had made that passage, which he described in *The Return of the Prodigal Son*, to becoming the father. He laughed more easily and full-heartedly. He was more relaxed."[162]

Nouwen sheds further light on how he was doing in a letter he wrote to his community in 1993: "In general I am feeling quite well and alive and am quite excited about my life at Daybreak. . . . Although I do feel I am quite busy at present I do not feel overburdened or overstretched."[163] He goes on to explain that he intends to only accept invitations that keep him close to the community.[164] He would accept invitations further afield only if it was as a messenger of L'Arche. He undertook to always travel with a core member as a sign of his commitment to Daybreak.

Nouwen wrote, "I realize how important it is to be a member of Daybreak and to be well held by the community."[165] His talks and retreats were to be either for other L'Arche communities or to fundraise for a new spirituality center for Daybreak. He would teach again but this time with co-teachers from the Daybreak community.

Nouwen had found home and intended to stay there. He understood that part of being the father was to be present to his community. Yet it is also true that to the end, Nouwen struggled with the tension of discerning the meaning of so many calls coming from around the world. The lure of new adventures never truly left him.

His Writing Vocation

In that same letter in which Nouwen details his need and hope to dedicate himself to Daybreak, he describes his call to write. He hoped to take a sabbatical from 1995 to 1996 to focus on it. He says, "I continue to feel that writing is what I most like to do. I feel increasingly a desire to write and I presently realize that I am delaying a lot of writing because of many other important activities. But I hope that, as I move towards the sabbatical year, there will be more and more space to write. I also very much want this writing to be writing that I share with the members of Daybreak so that it is really fruit of my being here."[166]

We can trace this renewed commitment back to *The Return of the Prodigal Son*. Nouwen felt that his experience of the painting and everything that he learned from it needed to be translated and shared with others. He had discovered a new place inside himself, the place "where God chose to dwell," and he wanted to write from that place. It was a vocational call that had always been there but was now more urgent: "I have a new vocation now. It is the vocation to speak and write from that place back into the many places of my own and other people's restless lives. I have to kneel before the Father, put my ear against his chest and listen, without interruption, to the heartbeat of God" (*Prodigal Son*, 15).

This is a remarkable declaration, which he would go on to take very seriously. Between 1992 and his death in 1996, Nouwen would write eleven more books. These include *Life of the Beloved*, published the same year as *The Return of the Prodigal Son*, detailing life after claiming divine son or daughtership; *Our Greatest Gift*, about death and dying; *Here and Now* and *Bread for the Journey*, two books that summarize his spiritual teachings to date; and *Adam: God's Beloved*, a testament to the gifts of a man with severe handicaps in Nouwen's own life.[167]

His writing became more cogent. *The Path* series is in fact four very short booklets, but each is a powerful expression of his spiritual vision.[168]

Nouwen's journey with the painting led him to claim his authority as a prophetic witness to God's presence in our lives. It was an authority that emerged from claiming his sonship and his passage to fatherhood.

Nouwen as Father

Be compassionate as your Father is compassionate.
(Luke 6:36)

Before Nouwen could become the father, he had to become the son. The two are inextricably linked. One of the obstacles to claiming his divine birthright was resistance to receiving love. In fact, an inability to accept love from God would continue long after the book was published. He confessed, "I am still not free enough to let myself be held completely in the safe embrace of the Father. In many ways I am still moving toward the center. I am still like the prodigal: travelling, preparing speeches, anticipating how it will be when I finally reach my Father's house" (*Prodigal Son*, 13).

At another level, he knew that his life was different now. He knew that, though the struggles would continue, he was on his way: "I have left the distant country and come to feel the nearness of love" (*Prodigal Son*, 13).

Nouwen called it a journey toward the light. He hadn't reached the final destination, but he now knew the way. This is significant. Nouwen shows us that to claim our sonship or daughtership is not a one-time event. It is a movement. Indeed, it is a constant leaving and returning. Yet the leaving is different now. It is not a rejection; it does not create distance, but is a choice. It is freedom.[169]

The same can be said of Nouwen's claim of spiritual fatherhood. He is candid with how difficult this vocational call is for him, even asking, "How can I choose what seems so contrary to all my needs?" (*Prodigal Son*, 129). Astonishingly, he chooses it anyway.

My people, whether handicapped or not, are not looking for another peer, another playmate, not even another brother. They seek a father who can bless and forgive without needing them in the way they need him. I see clearly the truth of my vocation to be a father; at the same time it seems to me almost impossible to follow it. I don't want to stay home while everyone goes out, whether driven by their many desires or their many angers. I feel these same impulses and want to run around like others do! But who is going to be home when they return—tired, exhausted, excited, disappointed, guilty, or ashamed? Who is going to convince them that, after all is said and done, there is a safe place to return to and receive an embrace? If it is not I, who is it going to be? (*Prodigal Son*, 124).

These are not rhetorical questions. Nouwen knows that the time has come for him to step up. Stories from people who knew Nouwen, then, help us understand the fruit of this radical choice.

One story is from Wendy Lywood, an Anglican priest mentioned previously, who was also an assistant at Daybreak during these crucial years. Lywood describes Nouwen comforting core member Michael Arnett after the death of Arnett's brother Adam, Nouwen's handicapped friend.

It was not so much what he said but the way his whole being became compassion. It seemed to me that both Michael and Henri were profoundly incarnational—Michael's pain and Henri's compassion were both experienced in the fullness of their humanity. In the Gospels when we are told that Jesus had compassion for the people, the Greek word used means that he was moved in his guts. Henri was following in the footsteps of Jesus in being such a compassionate pastor—he didn't hold back in fear, he didn't need to keep a professional distance.[170]

Another story is from Siobhan Keogh, also an assistant at Daybreak at this time. Keogh asked Nouwen to "adopt" her, and after careful reflection Nouwen agreed. She shares,

Henri loved me like a daughter—a beloved daughter in whom he was well pleased (Well, at times.) He took great care of me. Many have commented on his lack of homemaking skills. But over his years at Daybreak he learned much, and I was a recipient of the benefits of his growing knowledge. Our meetings were often over lunch, which he would carefully present on a lovely platter. During my year of intense darkness he did a great deal for me. When he heard that my cousin had committed suicide he called me up instantly. He wanted me to come to Dayspring to rest and be in his company. I replied that I had family commitments and mourning periods to attend to. "Fine, but come up after those," he said. Though there was no empty guest room, he set up the sofa bed in the library office. Tears still well up in my eyes when I remember how graciously and tenderly he arranged my room that night, comforting me amidst my fears and tears.[171]

The final story, about blessing people, comes from Nouwen himself. He recounts it in his book *Life of the Beloved*. One day, a disabled community member named Janet came to him and asked for a blessing. Nouwen, distracted by other things, quickly traced the sign of the cross on her forehead. "No," she protested. "That is not good enough. I want a real blessing!" Nouwen realized that she was looking for something personal. He promised her that at the next prayer service he would have a special blessing for her.

At the end of the prayer service, with about thirty people sitting in a circle on the floor, he announced, "Janet has asked me for a special blessing." He didn't quite know what she expected, but her next move left no doubt. She walked up to him, wrapped her arms around him, and said, "That's better, Henri." As he embraced her in return, her slight form almost disappeared in the folds of the white robe he wore while leading worship.

As they held each other, Nouwen said,

Janet, I want you to know that you are God's Beloved Daughter. You are precious in God's eyes. Your beautiful smile, your kindness to the people in your house, and all the good things you do show what a beautiful human being you are. I know you feel a little low these days and that there is some sadness in your heart, but I want you to remember who you are: a very special person, deeply loved by God and all the people who are here with you.

Janet raised her head and looked at him. Her beaming smile told him that she had received the blessing.

As Janet returned to her place, another woman raised her hand. She too wanted a blessing. She stood up and embraced Nouwen too, laying her face against his chest. After that, many more of the disabled members of the community took their turn, coming up for the same sort of blessing.

Finally, one of the assistants, a twenty-four-year-old college student, raised his hand and asked, "And what about me?" John was a big, burly young man, an athlete. Nouwen did the same with him, wrapping his arms around him and saying, "John, it is so good that you are here. You are God's Beloved Son. . . ." John looked back with tears in his eyes and simply said, "Thank you, thank you very much."[172]

This is a poignant story of how far Nouwen had moved along his journey to fatherhood. But, as with his journey to sonship, being the father was a lifelong struggle. He now knew where home was, but he couldn't always stay there. Unlike in typical hero stories, he does not satisfy us with a perfect ending.

Nouwen's life after *The Return of the Prodigal Son* continued to get busier. The restlessness he experienced earlier in life never left him completely. He still struggled with his longing for affection. He still longed for a sense of safety. Nouwen's account of his inner anguish written during his sabbatical and final year shows that in spite of the deep insights that came through "living the painting," he continued to carry his wounds through his life. In a journal entry from his final year he would write:

The feeling of being abandoned is always around the corner. I keep being surprised at how quickly it rears its ugly head. Yesterday I experienced that nasty feeling in my innermost being. Just raw anxiety, seemingly disconnected from anything. . . . Talking lessened my anxiety and I felt peaceful again. No one can ever heal this wound, but when I can talk about it with a good friend I feel better. . . . It is such a familiar wound. . . . Perhaps it is a gateway to my salvation, a door to glory, and a passage to freedom! I am aware that this wound of mine is a gift in disguise (*Sabbatical Journey*, 24–25).

Needing a New "Painting"

Nouwen's spiritual adventure started with the Rembrandt painting, but it couldn't take him all the way. Our hero, our friend, our guide is still in the struggle. As much as he was able to share the blessings of the father, he still yearned for the things of a child: to be held, to be safe, to be free. He needed a new image of God for this leg of his journey.

And he found one. This one was not a painting, or a person, or a Russian icon. It was alive and moving. It was the trapeze troupe the Flying Rodleighs. In a letter to a friend dated December 2, 1994, Nouwen wrote,

> The "Flying Rodleighs" express some of the deepest human desires. The desire to fly freely, and the desire to be safely caught. The act in a way is an expression of the human spirit, as it is incarnate in the athletic bodies of the trapeze artists. When I saw them for the first time, I had a feeling that they expressed one of my deepest inner longings to be totally free, as well as totally safe.[173]

Nouwen was transformed by the painting. His life changed. People around him were changed. But in the years following, he was still on his way home, and we can take comfort in this. Nouwen teaches that we can be spiritually mature and still have moments of being the prodigal son or the elder daughter. We can bless people and still yearn to be blessed. Nouwen shows us that what matters most is that we claim over and over to walk the path toward home. We may struggle for the rest of our lives, but we know where we are going and we know whose and what we are: a beloved child of God.

Christmas 1990 with Sue Mosteller, Patsy Ramsay, and Elizabeth Buckley at the Dayspring, L'Arche Daybreak

Henri Nouwen trying the trapeze with the Flying Rodleighs, 1993

Henri Nouwen's birth as a clown, 1992. Photograph
includes Mary Egan with child (left) and Sue Mosteller
(right).

Chapter 6 ∽
The Enduring Power of
The Return of the Prodigal Son

A classic is a book that has never finished saying what it has to say.

—Italo Calvino[174]

Henri Nouwen boarded a plane in Toronto for Amsterdam on September 16, 1996. He was headed to Saint Petersburg to see for a second time the original Rembrandt painting that had had such a profound effect on him. He was just finishing a sabbatical year that was as busy as any in his life. He had crisscrossed the ocean to Europe and across North America dozens of times, traveling thousands of kilometers for talks, funerals, weddings, political events, spiritual direction, and pastoral duties at Daybreak. He still managed to find time to write; he had six manuscripts in varying stages of completion by sabbatical's end.[175]

The impetus to see the painting again came from Jan van den Bosch, an evangelical media celebrity in Holland and the owner of Company Media Productions. Van den Bosch wanted to tell the story of Nouwen and his book in a filmed documentary. A visit to the Rembrandt painting at the Hermitage in Saint Petersburg was to be an important moment in the film.

After landing in Amsterdam, Nouwen took a train to Hilversuum, a half hour to the east, where he had booked a room at Hotel Lapershoek, a quaint, typically Dutch establishment that had long been a family favorite. He and his father had stayed there many times. By the time Nouwen checked in he was exhausted and told the front desk he was going to lie down before dinner.

A few moments after closing the door to his room he called down to reception to say he needed to see a doctor. He was having chest pains. Within minutes an ambulance arrived and the attendants assessed that he needed to go to the hospital immediately.

The stairs in the hotel were too narrow for an ambulance stretcher and Nouwen had to be lowered out the window by crane to the ambulance a few flights below.

At the hospital he was told he was having a heart attack. His family was called, and his father, brothers Paul and Laurent, and sister Laurien quickly made their way to the hospital.

At first, Nouwen seemed to stabilize. Nathan Ball, who flew in from Canada on September 20, four days after Nouwen was hospitalized, found Nouwen smiling and talkative, looking forward to his return to Daybreak in a few weeks. Nouwen even felt strong enough to walk Ball to the hospital entrance to say goodbye. His last words: "If I die tell everyone I am grateful. Enormously grateful. Tell everyone that."

In the early hours of his sixth night in the hospital, Nouwen had a second heart attack. He died alone in his room; everyone assumed he was recovering and needed his rest. He was sixty-four years old. He had outlived his Dutch confrère Rembrandt by one year.

Henri Nouwen and Rembrandt Harmenszoon van Rijn both completed their masterworks near the end of their lives. Rembrandt finished his prodigal son painting two years before his death in 1701; Nouwen published *The Return of the Prodigal Son* four years before his death in 1996. The power of both works derives from their creators' difficult lives of struggle, as well as their artistic maturity. The painting and the book are spiritual testaments to hard-won wisdom.

There is another commonality between these Dutch brothers. Both Nouwen and Rembrandt were masters of self-portraits: Nouwen through words, Rembrandt with pigments. Both were able to survey themselves "without vanity and with the utmost sincerity."[176]

Rembrandt painted nearly a hundred self-portraits over his lifetime, each one with eyes that told the story. As a young painter, his eyes were defiant, cocky even, but as the tragedies of loss accumulated, the eyes became more penetrating. They looked out at the viewer unmasked. Like Nouwen, he sensed his belovedness even while the world abandoned him. While staying true to his increasingly outdated style, the self-portraits became more impressionistic, suggesting a spiritual dimension or higher truth behind the visible world.

Nouwen's self-portraits, told through his published diaries, speeches, and books, are about self-discovery. He was painfully aware of his own wounds and used his powers of penetration to unmask the "gift" in his pain. Life itself was the laboratory for self-knowledge. As he aged, his writing became increasingly candid. His diary from Winnipeg, which was published as *The Inner Voice of Love*, is a deeply personal portrait of his depression and quest for God in the midst of it.

Yet what sets apart these works as masterpieces is portraiture of a different kind—God's. Both Nouwen and Rembrandt caught a glimpse of a loving, extravagant, forgiving God and used their witness to give us an image of the ineffable that consoles and heals.

As masterful as the book is, however, it does demand hearts that are ready and prepared to receive its wisdom. *The Return of the*

Prodigal Son tends to come to people at the right time. This is a book that readers find when they need it—usually when they are on their knees. It is also one of those rare books that reveals something new with each reading. Perhaps this is the true criterion of a spiritual classic: like Scripture, it changes with each reading. As we mature, more is revealed. It is a classic because, as Italo Calvino defines it, it never finishes saying what it has to say.

The book is compelling because it is such a good story. Nouwen faces obstacles we can relate to and overcomes them. Nouwen is our everyperson. He is us, but perhaps slightly braver. He goes out ahead and provides us a road map so we can undertake our own journey of self-discovery. Moreover, he shows us how to make a commitment to this valuable but invisible path. He gives us a template for making a vow to claim the truth: "Claiming the truth is the inner work that I commit to today and it leads me to see that I must respond to life's interruptions from a new perspective. It is radical for me, involving an almost constant effort to overcome my resistance to overturn old patterns. That is why I have resolved to give time to reflect on this invitation, to pray often in gratitude and petition, and to find the necessary support and accountability for my commitment" (*Home Tonight*, 74).

Nouwen shows us that we can regroup and live with more purpose, more confidence, and more love. As readers, we sense the great gift in this. It heals us in our deepest, most shame-filled places, simply by bringing his own vulnerabilities into the light.

That is not to say that even while we are consoled by the book we aren't challenged by it as well. Not all of us will be ready to accept the "dreadful emptiness" of spiritual fatherhood or motherhood that Nouwen so fearlessly claims for himself. But Nouwen shows us that this is okay. He hesitated, too. In fact, as we've seen, his call to fatherhood came quite early on in his journey with the painting, yet he didn't answer it. He was in Winnipeg at Homes for Growth when Mosteller's letter reached him. She invited him then to step up as father, but nearly three years later, Mosteller had to remind him again: "I still feel like you are not claiming where you are," she wrote.

Even at the end of the book, Nouwen is tentative about the great challenge ahead of him, but what inspires is that he is ready and willing to embrace it. He knows he is going to struggle. He knows it is going to touch his wound of loneliness and self-rejection. But he does it anyway. Perhaps this is why readers feel such an intimacy with this book. We have very real choices to make, too, but Nouwen is there making it all seem possible. Nouwen's voice is invitational. It is gentle and kind. It is as though he tenderly reaches out and removes the mask we wear to protect ourselves and says, "You can do this." But it is our choice.

The Return of the Prodigal Son is a story of Nouwen's journey from a needy, anxious university professor into a needy, anxious pastor, but he has grown in consciousness. He is not living his neediness the same way. The light of awareness has entered the dark places and changed them. He shows us that the path to our full humanity is not linear. It is a movement that leans forward and then pitches back. This is all right.

But, as much as Nouwen teaches us about the value of the struggle, he also teaches us that we can transform our suffering into something generative for ourselves and for others. The book touches us because we can suddenly see the nobility of our lives. We, in all our imperfections, are called to be compassionate as God is compassionate. The idea that we are divine as God is divine is audacious, but as Nouwen says, this book, and Rembrandt's painting, are not saying anything that Jesus hasn't already said in the New Testament: "All of the Gospel is there. All of my life is there. All of the lives of my friends are there. The painting has become a mysterious window through which I can step into the Kingdom of God. It is like a huge gate that allows me to move to the other side of existence and look from there back into the odd assortment of people and events that make up my life" (*Prodigal Son*, 14).

The book is for us what the painting was for Nouwen. It allows us to look back over our life and see it with different eyes. It gives us a new vision. We look at our relationships, our actions, our feelings, and thought patterns in a new light.

We start seeing with the eyes of our soul. We know how to do it because, in fact, *The Return of the Prodigal Son* is as much a portrait of Nouwen's soul as it is of God. Nouwen has articulated the terrain of his innermost being. While much attention is given to our physical bodies and our psychological state of mind, this book asks us to draw our attention inward. Nouwen introduces us to a place within where we may have never visited before. We learn to ask, "What do I have to do?" rather than "What do I want to do?" We wonder, "Is there meaning in my life?" rather than "Am I happy?" Nouwen's book calls for no less than our conversion to God's way of thinking. We are asked to stop imposing "the economy of the temporal on the unique order of the divine" (*Prodigal Son*, 98).

Ronald Rolheiser, a writer and catholic priest, defines a mystic as someone who gives you words for what you already know. By this definition, Nouwen was a mystic and *The Return of the Prodigal Son* is a mystical text in the tradition of Thérèse de Lisieux and John of the Cross. Reading *The Return of the Prodigal Son* is to be introduced to ourselves. Nouwen introduces us to our own depth. He shows us that we are more than our thoughts and feelings. We have a deep center that connects with something beyond ourselves.

Mystics are also often prophets. Nouwen's editor Conrad Wieczorek saw this aspect of Nouwen after reading a draft of the manuscript in 1990. Conrad wrote,

If the role of the prophet is to remind me of my duty of who I am and to bring me back (call me) home to obedience and love, stuff you have already written has served this function for me. My reaction to your writings from the beginning was: This man speaks with authority—not like the psychologists and social workers—This man knows whereof he speaks. In telling your own story, you told mine, in sharing your own hope, you spoke to my deepest desires, and, because of this, I became more or less willing to exercise the disciplines you suggested.[177]

Nouwen felt the call of the prophet himself. In some of the best lines of the book he says, "I know now that I have to speak from eternity into time, from lasting joy into the passing realities of our short existence in this world, from the house of love into the houses of fear, from God's abode into the dwellings of human beings. I am well aware of the enormity of this vocation. Still, I am confident that it is the only way for me" (*Prodigal Son*, 15). He concludes, "One could call it the 'prophetic vision': looking at people and this world through the eyes of God" (*Prodigal Son*, 15).

As readers of *The Return of the Prodigal Son*, we trust Nouwen. We trust him because he shares his vulnerability with us. As much as he can make the confident claim of prophet, he does so from a place of much suffering. Like Rembrandt, who "must have died many deaths and cried many tears to have painted a portrait of God in such humility" (*Prodigal Son*, 19), Nouwen has an authenticity that we recognize and want to emulate. What touches us is how generous Nouwen was with his life and how deeply he saw into things. Nouwen *sees* Rembrandt and his painting. It was his commitment to live his pains that made it possible for him to see the shadow and light of another person with such depth. Compassion gave him the eyes to see so clearly what many of us might miss.

A prophet holds up a mirror to us and to the societal norms of our day. Nouwen does this with a psychologist's insight but also with deep humility. He is not above it all. He gently points out what is wrong with our society and why we may be anxious or unfulfilled, by articulating his own path through it.

As readers of *The Return of the Prodigal Son*, we know this inner imperative to grow up. Some of us just don't know how to do it. Nouwen gives us an example. He doesn't want to give up his childish ways any more than we do, but his encounter with Rembrandt and his painting shows him that he must step through his fears and claim his paternity. Paradoxically, he does this by simultaneously claiming his identity as a child of God: "As long as we belong to this world, we will remain subject to its competitive ways and expect to be rewarded for all the good we do. But when we belong to God, who loves us without conditions, we can live as he does. The great conversion called for by Jesus is to move from belonging to the world to belonging to God" (*Prodigal Son*, 117).

We no longer hear these words as a renunciation of the world and physical pleasure, but as a way to live in the world in full freedom. Maturity means living with a whole new set of values. Nouwen wakes us up to what is deepest inside us. Like Nouwen, we won't be perfect. We may continue to vacillate between being the younger and elder son, but we have a new way of living.

Perhaps even more important than showing us our societal reluctance to grow up is Nouwen's insight into his own, and by extension our, propensity for self-rejection. By naming self-rejection and connecting it to our reluctance to receive God, Nouwen touches on a core truth about many of us: we have deep wells of unworthiness. He names a very hidden but also very corrosive aspect of modern society that affects many people.

Nouwen reassures us that it doesn't need to be this way. Like him, we can "choose for the light" (*Prodigal Son*, 108) and allow ourselves to be loved. In the parable, love is always there. Nouwen shows us how to soften our boundaries and open to this field of loving. For many readers this is transformative and profoundly healing.

Self-rejection is closely tied to our image of God. By healing our relationship with God, Nouwen helps heal our relationship to ourselves. He begins this process by describing God as many of us know God—as threatening and fearsome. Then, through Rembrandt's painting, Nouwen gives us a new icon to heal this image of the divine.

Nouwen introduces us to a God that, far from rejecting us or acting out revenge for our wrongdoings, gives up power to give us the freedom to love or reject love as we want. God's love, Nouwen shows us, "cannot force, constrain, push, or pull" (*Prodigal Son*, 89). To this free, gentle, invitational, and loving God that Nouwen offers to us, so many are drawn.

Nouwen rehabilitates God from a "boss" to a vessel of unconditional love. Seen in this way, *The Return of the Prodigal Son* is a critique of patriarchy and the ways it has distorted our image of fathers. This has two interrelated effects. The first is to speak into the current issue of toxic masculinity and offer a new way of being a man. The second is to present to us a vision in which binary, gendered, literal views of God are no longer needed.

Father Figures and Toxic Masculinity

Nouwen refers to patriarchy by name only once. We find it in the chapter on the father. It comes up as Nouwen reflects on how the father in the parable is generous: "The way the younger son is given robe, ring, and sandals, and welcomed home with sumptuous celebration, as well as the way the elder son is urged to accept his unique place in his father's heart and to join his younger brother around the table, make it very clear that all boundaries of patriarchal behavior are broken through" (*Prodigal Son*, 122).

It is not just the Father who was breaking boundaries. Isn't this entire work a gentle, but powerful, revocation of the patriarchal system? Nouwen (and Rembrandt) shows us that being a man does not mean being all-powerful, stoical, unemotional, or invincible. Instead, these works show us that to be man, woman, human means to be powerless, honest, emotional, and vulnerable. We can and must grieve openly, give generously, and forgive endlessly.[178]

Seeing our fellow human beings as competitors is a key aspect of patriarchy. There are winners and there are losers, and we all must fight our way to the top. Nouwen struggled with this aspect of the patriarchal system. A particular obstacle to spiritual fatherhood was giving up control—more specifically, giving up his competitive side. He confessed how difficult this was to do: "I must trust that I am capable of becoming the Father I am called to be" (*Prodigal Son*, 120).

Nouwen had learned his competitive skills from his father, and no doubt this lineage of competition from father to child goes back generations. But Nouwen breaks through this limited way of seeing fatherhood and becomes a different kind of parent. He shifts our understanding of parenthood from a fear-based model to a love-centered one.

By healing our image of God the Father, Nouwen also heals our image of masculinity. Suddenly, we have a new vision for what it means to care for and love our children. Patriarchy teaches all of us, but men in particular, to hide weakness and vulnerability. But we are called to be compassionate as God is compassionate. We can only do this by entering into pain and suffering—in our lives and then the lives of others. Far from competing with other people, we are called to love them, expecting nothing in return.

A Both/And God

On the one hand, *The Return of the Prodigal Son* is about healing our image of God. Nouwen, through Rembrandt, gives us a new portrait of God. He teaches us to imagine and internalize this loving Father in our innermost being and learn to receive his love. At the same time, in a subtle way, Nouwen is leading us away from literal imagery.

Nouwen's God is nongendered. In addition to drawing our attention to the hands of the father in the painting as both masculine and feminine, he writes, "It is the first and everlasting love of a God who is Father as well as Mother. . . . Jesus' whole life and preaching had only one aim: to reveal this inexhaustible, unlimited motherly and fatherly love of his God and to show the way to let that love guide every part of our daily lives" (*Prodigal Son*, 102).

Nouwen is suggesting more than just a shift away from strict gender norms. He is also moving toward a God who can't be contained in one image. The God of *The Return of the Prodigal Son* holds opposites. God is both/and.

God is both an interior God (we are the "place that God has chosen to dwell"[179]) and a cosmic God who links us to the past, present, and future. God is eternal and also "still."[180] We are on our way, and we have already returned. We are not to be *like* the father but to *be* the father. We are not finding home. We are home. Moreover, just as we have already returned, we are also emerging.

God, in Nouwen's understanding, is unity: "Everything comes together here: Rembrandt's story, humanity's story and God's story. Time and eternity intersect; approaching death and everlasting life touch each other. Sin and forgiveness embrace; the human and the divine become one" (*Prodigal Son*, 88).

Nouwen is speaking from the vantage point of *kairos*. Kairos, a Greek word for time, was understood by Nouwen to mean "the opportunity to change your heart." From this time zone he can see the prodigal son painting as a portrait of the child becoming the father and the father becoming the child. Here, in kairos time, resentment dissolves into gratitude and what is finished is becoming.

Perhaps this portrait of "both/and" as it pertains to God, time, and indeed the entire human condition is the most prescient, challenging, and least understood aspect of this book.[181]

An Unfinished Story

Unlike a fairy tale, the parable provides no happy
ending. Instead, it leaves us face to face with one of
life's hardest spiritual choices: to trust or not to trust
God's all-forgiving love. (Henri Nouwen)[182]

For all its cosmic perspective, the parable of *The Return of the Prodigal Son* is also a human story, and one that isn't quite finished. Does the elder son join the celebration? Does the younger son stay home once his belly is full? Does the mother emerge from the shadows and show her face? The parable is open-ended, as are all of our stories, as indeed is the story of all creation. The unfinished parable parallels Nouwen's unfinished spiritual journey.

One way of understanding this open-endedness is to think of it as a story about relationships—between parent and child, between siblings, between members of a household, between our true self and God. By gazing into the painting as deeply as he did, and living out the teaching of parable as imagined by Rembrandt, Nouwen reconciles many important relationships in his life—with his father, with his friend Nathan Ball, with God, and with himself. But as impressive as this is, and as informative as it is for our own versions of reconciliation, the painting did not heal his broken relationship with his body. In *The Return of the Prodigal Son*, Nouwen writes about our body as God's home, but even after his long journey with the painting, he was still struggling to live this in the flesh.

Rembrandt's prodigal son could only take Henri Nouwen so far on this aspect of his journey. But just at the moment that he had exhausted the meaning of "his" painting, the trapeze act was "given" to him.[183]

At first, he couldn't articulate why the trapeze affected him so profoundly. But he knew that, like his reaction to the Rembrandt painting, this was another "gate" to glimpse the mystery of God. He knew it held an "important secret" that would reveal itself if he remained "faithful to [his] intuition."[184]

What was the secret? To befriend his body. The trapeze metaphor pushed Nouwen to consider that his deepest, yes, most difficult, search was for a relationship with his physical self. The trapeze act struck him with such force because it asked him to consider what incarnation really meant for him: "Seeing the Rodleighs catapulted me into a new consciousness. There in the air I saw the artistic realization of my deepest yearning. It was so intense that even today I do not dare to write about it because it requires a radical new step not only in my writing but also in my life" (*Sabbatical Journey*, 121–22).

We can only speculate, but what Nouwen might have seen there was a vision of unity, in which individuals form a whole, where through practice and discipline, risk and surrender, they create beauty and lift the human spirit. He saw artists who were using their bodies to give expression to the human endeavor of love and trust. He saw in them an incarnation of God's desire for our full expression of our humanity.

According to Sue Mosteller, Nouwen's friendship and care of his handicapped friend Adam Arnett prepared him to *see* the Flying Rodleighs the way he did. By washing Arnett, dressing him, brushing his teeth, holding him during a seizure, and other acts of tenderness, Nouwen went deeper into his own physical experience. His blessings manifested themselves in touch. Like the Father in the painting, he used his enormous hands to rest on people's shoulders in an embrace of comfort and encouragement. But years of denial and shame around his body continued to plague him. His captivation with the trapeze as an image signaled his readiness to enter into this part of his life journey and begin to heal it.

Like *The Return of the Prodigal Son*, this was another book that needed to be lived before it could be written, and Nouwen died before that could happen. His "circus book," however, remains his great unfinished work.[185] We can mourn this lost testament to his journey of fully accepting and living in his body; it would have been a story that was healing for so many. But we can also rejoice in the fullness of his completed work *The Return of the Prodigal Son*, for the "pearls of great price" that he was indeed able to share.

In the prologue to *The Return of the Prodigal Son*, Nouwen wonders how his "precious hours in the Hermitage would ever bear fruit" (*Prodigal Son*, 10). In the last paragraph, he answers his own question:

> When, four years ago, I went to Saint Petersburg to see Rembrandt's The Return of the Prodigal Son, I had little idea how much I would have to live what I then saw. I stand with awe at the place where Rembrandt brought me. He led me from the kneeling, disheveled young son to the standing, bent-over old father, from the place of being blessed to the place of blessing. As I look at my own aging hands, I know that they have been given to me to stretch out toward all who suffer, to rest upon the shoulders of all who come, and to offer the blessing that emerges from the immensity of God's love. (*Prodigal Son*, 129–30)

Nouwen is like the catcher on the trapeze, his hands stretched out to catch the flyer who leaves the safe platform trusting they will be caught. And Nouwen is also the flyer who is willing to take risks in all manner of ways. With his example, we can be emboldened to take our own flights of courage and grace. We, too, can risk it all when we trust in God's forgiving love.

Notes

Chapter One Notes 1–24

1 David Richo, *How to Be an Adult: A Handbook on Psychological and Spiritual Integration* (Mahwah, NJ: Paulist Press, 1991), 6–7.

2 Henri Nouwen, *[First Draft of the Prodigal Son]* (Henri Nouwen fonds, Accession files, Turner accession, the Henri J. M. Nouwen Archives and Research Collection, Accession 2010 63), 3.

3 Nouwen, *[First Draft of the Prodigal Son]*, 7.

4 Peter Naus in conversation with author, 2011.

5 Nouwen, *[First Draft of the Prodigal Son]*, 4.

6 The tour, "Interrupted Journey: Peacemaking in Nicaragua and Peru," took place between November and December 1983. It was arranged by the United States Catholic Mission Association.

7 Henri Nouwen to Richard, 1996 (Henri Nouwen fonds, Accession files, the Henri J. M. Nouwen Archives and Research Collection, Accession 2006 08).

8 Jean Vanier (1928-2019) was the co-founder of L'Arche, an intentional community built for and around people with intellectual disabilities. In February 2020, as this book was in the final stages of production, an inquiry was released by L'Arche International stating that Vanier had "manipulative sexual relationships'" with at least six women. Future explorations of Nouwen's life and work will likely re-evaluate the dynamic at play between Nouwen and Vanier in light of these revelations.

9 We can notice this same dynamic at play in 2020. Younger people sneer, "OK, boomer," partially in response to a perception that the climate emergency we are facing is a result of the older generations' wanton exploitation of the environment.

10 Henri Nouwen, "Generation Without Fathers," *Commonweal*, June 12, 1970, 287–94, reprinted in *Christian Education: Selections of Significance*, National Education Office, Canadian Catholic Conference, 65 (June 1, 1970): 7.

11 Laurence Freeman, "Daily Wisdom—Aspects of Love 3," World Community for Christian Meditation, February 6, 2019, http://www.wccm.org/sites/default/files/users/Audio/2014B%20Aspects%20of%20Love%203%20-Master2.pdf?mc_cid=eaea6d5d86&mc_eid=b70be51029.

12 Richard Rohr, "Changing Perspectives—Jesus and the Cross," Center for Action and Contemplation, February 5, 2019, https://cac.org/changing-perspectives-2019-02-05/.

13 Nouwen, *[First Draft of the Prodigal Son]*, 2.

14 Lily E. Clerx and Marinus H. Van Ijzendoorn, *Child Care in a Dutch Context: On the History, Current States and Evaluation of Nonmaternal Child Care in the Netherlands,* in *Child Care in Context,* ed. Michael E. Lamb, Kathleen J. Sternberg, Carl-Philip Hwang, and Anders G. Broberg (Hillsdale, NJ: Lawrence Eribaum, 1992), 63.

15 Two examples: "I kept being drawn by my love-hungry heart to deceptive ways of gaining a sense of self-worth" (*Prodigal Son,* 45); "The anguish of abandonment was so biting that it was hard, almost impossible, to believe that voice [of love]" (*Prodigal Son,* 45).

16 Recently Sipe played himself as an off-camera character in the film *Spotlight.* He died on August 8, 2018.

17 From A. W. Richard Sipe, "The Reality of Celibate Life: Reflections from Henri Nouwen," *National Catholic Reporter,* October 2010, https://www.ncronline.org/blogs/examining-crisis/reality-celibate-life-reflections-henri-nouwen.

18 Sipe, "Reality of Celibate Life."

19 Laurent Nouwen in conversation with author, 2012.

20 This article was published in his first book, *Intimacy: Pastoral Psychological Essays* (Notre Dame, IN: Fides, 1970). In it he argues that homosexuality is an aberrant mental state. This was removed in the 2nd edition after Nouwen's position changed on the subject due to the number of distressed letters he received from readers. He no longer viewed homosexuality as a mental illness.

21 Laurent Nouwen's conversation with author, September 2012.

22 Nouwen, *[First Draft of the Prodigal Son]*, 4.

23 As he stood before the painting in Russia he said, "I was deeply aware of the return, the return to the womb of the Divine Creator" (*Home Tonight,* 17).

24 John O'Donohue, *Anam Cara: A Book of Celtic Wisdom* (New York: HarperCollins, 1998), 26.

Chapter Two Notes 25–72

25 From "Returning" retreat, author's transcription notes, 15.

26 Part of Nouwen's energy for writing a book about icons came from the mother of Jean Vanier, Madame Pauline Vanier, whom Nouwen lived with while staying at La Ferme and whose devotion with icons influenced his own practice.

27 We might hear this as foreshadowing of *The Return of the Prodigal Son* when he says he hoped that through the Rembrandt masterpiece he would "one day be able to express what he most wanted to say about love" (*Prodigal Son,* 6).

28 Adapted from "Visio Divina," The Upper Room, https://www.upperroom.org/resources/visio-divina.

29 The painting hangs in the National Gallery of Canada.

30 Sue Mosteller, in conversation with author, May 2019.

31 Henri Nouwen, *Draft of Circus Diary*, Henri Nouwen fonds, Manuscript Series, Books and Articles, the Henri J. M. Nouwen Archives and Research Collection, chap. 2, p. 9, Box 23, File 1-1-1-67.

32 Nouwen, *Draft of Circus Diary*, 10.

33 Nouwen, *Draft of Circus Diary*, 9.

34 Nouwen, *Draft of Circus Diary*, 9–10.

35 Nouwen, *Draft of Circus Diary*, 10.

36 Henri Nouwen, letter to Jim Antal, May 30, 1976, published in Henri Nouwen, *Love, Henri: Letters on the Spiritual Life*, ed. Gabrielle Earnshaw (New York: Convergent, 2016), 21.

37 Many will argue that "pastor" was his foremost identity, and I wouldn't disagree. But his ministry was expressed through his artistic core.

38 Henri Nouwen, letter to Marcus, January 20, 1990, in *Love, Henri*, 247–48.

39 Henri Nouwen, *[First Draft of the Prodigal Son]*, Henri Nouwen fonds, Accession files, Turner accession, the Henri J. M. Nouwen Archives and Research Collection, Accession 2010 63, 33.

40 Nouwen, *[First Draft of the Prodigal Son]*, 36.

41 It should be noted that a similar analysis of Nouwen's attunement to listening/deafness could be a fruitful exercise. Nouwen wrote extensively about this aspect of the spiritual life. He frames the younger son's dilemma, for instance, as being "deaf" to the voice of love. Other examples could be found in the text.

42 From Nouwen's record of his meeting with Boisen in August 1964 in "Boisen," Henri Nouwen fonds, Manuscript Series, the Henri J. M. Nouwen Archives and Research Collection, Box 1, File 01-2.

43 Henri Nouwen, letter to Mark, September 4, 1982, in *Love, Henri*, 72.

44 Willem Berger was the assistant to Han Fortmann. Fortmann was a professor of the psychology of religion and culture at the Catholic University of Nijmegen (1957–1970). Author conversations with Peter Naus and Piet van Hooydonk in 2011.

45 Due to Freud's atheism and philosophical determinism there developed a great deal of animosity between psychoanalysis and Roman Catholicism (see Kevin Gillespie, "Psychology and American Catholicism After Vatican II: Currents, Cross-Currents and Confluences," *U.S. Historian* 25, no. 4, American Catholics and the Social Sciences [Fall 2007]: 117–31).

46 Pius XII, "On Psychotherapy and Religion," Encyclical Letter, 1953, Papal Encyclicals Online, http://www.papalencyclicals.net/pius12/p12psyre.htm.

47 Fortmann, Nouwen's thesis advisor, was the first chair of psychology of religion at the Catholic University of Nijmegen, which was established in 1956, just one year before Nouwen's ordination as a priest in 1957.

48 The specificity of this information is taken from Chris de Bono's doctoral thesis "An Exploration and Adaptation of Anton T. Boisen's Notion of the Psychiatric Chaplain in Responding to Current Issues in Clinical Chaplaincy" (PhD diss., University of St. Michael's College and the Pastoral Department of the Toronto School of Theology, 2012). Bono writes, "A careful reading of Nouwen's published material indicates that on four occasions he did cite strategically Boisen in three books, and wrote two articles on Boisen, all between 1968 and 1977. But for all intents and purposes, after that, published references to Boisen disappear" (p. 164).

49 These case studies document the patients Boisen cared for in the 1920s and 1930s as a chaplain.

50 Consider the scriptural passage: "You show that you are a letter from Christ, the result of our ministry written not with ink but with the spirit of the living God, not on tablets of stone but on tablets of human hearts" (2 Cor. 3:3 NIV).

51 Italics are mine. Boisen said this in a speech before the Chicago Council for Clinical Training in 1950; see Robert Leas, "The Biography of Anton Theophilus Boisen," Association for Clinical Pastoral Education, https://www.acpe.edu/pdf/History/The%20Biography%20of%20Anton%20Theophilus%20Boisen.pdf.

52 Nouwen spent time in rural pastorates of Alabama during the course of his Menninger studies.

53 As quoted in Robert D. Leas and John R. Thomas, "A Brief History," Association for Clinical Pastoral Education, https://www.acpe.edu/pdf/History/ACPE%20Brief%20History.pdf.

54 From Nouwen's record of his meeting with Boisen in August 1964. See "Boisen," the Henri J. M. Nouwen Archives and Research Collection, Box 1, File 01-2.

55 "Boisen," Nouwen Archives.

56 Nouwen to a friend, July 1996, in *Love, Henri*, xv.

57 Henri Nouwen on Boisen in his article "Anton T. Boisen and Theology Through Living Human Documents," *Pastoral Psychology* 19, no. 186 (September 1968): 50.

58 Carol Berry, *Learning from Henri Nouwen and Vincent Van Gogh: A Portrait of the Compassionate Life* (Downers Grove, IL: InterVarsity Press, 2019), xv.

59 Fragments of this play are held in the Henri J. M. Nouwen Archives and Research Collection at the University of St. Michael's College, University of Toronto.

60 From preface to *Encounters with Merton: Spiritual Reflections* (New York: Crossroad, 2005), 13, a revised edition of *Pray to Live: Thomas Merton; A Contemplative Critic* (Notre Dame, IN: Fides, 1972).

61 Jenkinson is now more known for his work with death and dying.

62 Although Nouwen did a thorough scholarly review of Rembrandt and the prodigal son painting in preparation for his book (and there are more footnotes in this work than any other), his intent was not a strict art history interpretation. He wrote from his heart, from the place of "divine seeing." *The Return of the Prodigal Son* has more in common with Augustine's *Confessions* than a treatise of art history. Nouwen is ultimately a pastor who uses his writing and teaching to help people on their journey.

63 After his first wife's death, Rembrandt had two subsequent marriages. He had his second wife committed to an insane asylum for twelve years and later married a much younger woman who bore his only child to survive him; she died six years before Rembrandt.

64 Much of the information about Boisen in this section comes from Boisen scholar Glenn H. Asquith Jr., assistant professor of pastoral theology, Moravian Theology Seminary, Bethlehem, PA, including "The Case Study Method of Anton T. Boisen," *Journal of Pastoral Care* 34, no. 2 (June 1980): 82–94, and "Anton T. Boisen and the Study of 'Living Human Documents,'" *Journal of Presbyterian History* 60, no. 3 (1980): 244–65.

65 Glenn Asquith Jr., "Anton T. Boisen: A Vision for All Ages" (CPSP plenary address, Chicago, Illinois, March 15, 2015), http://www.cpsp .org/pastoralreportarticles/3779024.

66 Henri Nouwen, "Pastoral Supervision in Historical Perspective" (Henri Nouwen fonds, Nouwen's Education Records and Study Documents, Menninger Clinic Records, The Henri J. M. Nouwen Archives and Research Collection Box 287, File 1-8-4-306), 69.

67 Henri Nouwen, "Pastoral Supervision in Historical Perspective," 70.

68 This is a based on a quote from Boisen as cited by Nouwen in his unpublished work "Anton T. Boisen and the Study of Theology Through Living Human Documents" (Henri Nouwen fonds, Manuscripts, Books and Articles, the Henri J. M. Nouwen Archives and Research Collection, Box 1, File 1-1-1-05), 52–53.

69 Henri Nouwen, "Anton T. Boisen and the Study of Theology Through Living Human Documents," 52–53.

70 See Leas, "Biography."

71 Arthur Boers, "L'Arche and the Heart of God" in Henri Nouwen, *The Road to Peace: Writings on Peace and Justice*, edited by John Dear

(Maryknoll, NY: Orbis, 1998), 156. Originally published as "Faces of Faith: Henri Nouwen," *The Other Side*, September-October 1989, 14–19.

72 Boers, "L'Arche and the Heart of God," 156.

Chapter Three Notes 73–137

73 Henri Nouwen, *[First Draft of the Prodigal Son]* (Henri Nouwen fonds, Accession files, Turner accession, the Henri J. M. Nouwen Archives and Research Collection, Accession 2010 63), 18.

74 In a letter to Carol Plantinga Mead, from November 26, 1985, Nouwen refers to the prodigal son and says he "very much wants to write about it" (in Carol Plantinga fonds, the Henri J. M. Nouwen Archives and Research Collection, file 2010 23 01 03).

75 Arthur Boers, "L'Arche and the Heart of God," in Henri Nouwen, *The Road to Peace: Writings on Peace and Justice*, ed. John Dear (Maryknoll, NY: Orbis, 1998), 153.

76 Joe Egan, letter to Henri Nouwen, December 4, 1985 (Henri Nouwen fonds, the Henri J. M. Archives and Research Collection, File 4954). For a digital copy of this letter see https://usmccollections.library.utoronto .ca/islandora/object/usmc2%3A1187.

77 Boers, "L'Arche and the Heart of God," 154.

78 Henri Nouwen, letter to Joe Egan, February 8, 1986 (Henri Nouwen fonds, the Henri J. M. Nouwen Archives and Research Collection, File 4934). For a digital copy of this letter see https://usmccollections.library .utoronto.ca/islandora/object/usmc%3A67.

79 Massie is an Episcopal priest, writer, activist, and American politician.

80 Interview with Robert Kinloch Massie by Sue Mosteller (the Henri Nouwen Oral History Project fonds, the Henri J. M. Nouwen Archives and Research Collection., SR2007 68 42 30 vol. 1).

81 Interview with Robert Kinloch Massie by Sue Mosteller.

82 Interview with Robert Kinloch Massie by Sue Mosteller.

83 Interview with Robert Kinloch Massie by Sue Mosteller (the Henri Nouwen Oral History Project fonds, the Henri J. M. Nouwen Archives and Research Collection., SR2007 68 42 30 vol. 1).

84 Robert Massie, "God's Restless Servant," in *Befriending Life: Encounters with Henri Nouwen*, ed. Beth Porter (New York: Doubleday, 2001), 16.

85 Boers, "L'Arche and Heart of God," 154–55.

86 Nouwen writes a moving account about this uneasy transition from academia to L'Arche in *Adam: God's Beloved*, published posthumously (Maryknoll, NY: Orbis, 1996).

87 Henri Nouwen, letter to Sue Mosteller, February 1988 (the Henri J. M. Nouwen Archives and Research Collection, Accession 2002 86, File 12).

88 Joe Egan, letter to Henri Nouwen, January 1, 1988 (the Henri J. M. Nouwen Archives and Research Collection, Accession 2002 86, Folder 12), 2.

89 Henri Nouwen, letter to Mosteller, February 18, 1988 (the Henri J. M. Nouwen Archives and Research Collection, Accession 2002 86, Folder 12).

90 Henri Nouwen, letter to Mosteller, February 1988 (the Henri J. M. Nouwen Archives and Research Collection, Accession 2002 86, Folder 12).

91 Nouwen, [First Draft of the Prodigal Son], 4.

92 Thomas Philippe (1905-1993), a Dominican priest, was the co-founder of L'Arche with Jean Vanier. In 2014, an inquiry concluded that he, like Vanier, had committed acts of serious sexual abuse against multiple women. Both men were revered in their lifetimes. Mosteller, reflecting common sentiments of the time, refers to them as men to be emulated.

93 Sue Mosteller, letter to Henri Nouwen, February 28, 1988 (the Henri J. M. Nouwen Archives and Research Collection, Accession 2002 86, Folder 12).

94 Henri Nouwen, letter to Sue Mosteller, March 4, 1988 (the Henri J. M. Nouwen Archives and Research Collection, Accession 2002 86, Folder 12).

95 Sue Mosteller, letter to Henri Nouwen and Nathan Ball, July 12, 1988 (the Henri J. M. Nouwen Archives and Research Collection, Accession 2012 86, Folder 12).

96 Nouwen, [First Draft of the Prodigal Son], 18.

97 Nouwen, [First Draft of the Prodigal Son], 21.

98 Connie Ellis, letter to Gordon Turner, February 26, 1988 (Henri Nouwen fonds, Accession files, Turner accession, the Henri J. M. Nouwen Archives and Research Collection, Accession 2010 63).

99 This is the "Returning" retreat mentioned earlier.

100 Henri Nouwen, letter to Daybreak Council, January 20, 1989 (the Henri J. M. Nouwen Archives and Research Collection, Accession 2002 86, Folder 12), 1–2.

101 Nouwen, letter to Daybreak Council, January 20, 1989, 2.

102 Nouwen, letter to Daybreak Council, January 20, 1989, 3.

103 Henri Nouwen, letter to Phillip Zaeder, July 7, 1989 (Henri Nouwen fonds, General Files, the Henri J. M. Nouwen Archives and Research Collection, Box 116, File 6605).

104 In a letter to Paula Kilcoyne, a fellow Daybreak community member, he wrote, "I recently returned from two months in France where

I stayed in the Trosly community to work on a book about the prodigal son. I was able to complete the first draft and am happy with the time the community gave me, but it is also good to be back in Daybreak. It was in Trosly that I became aware how much I really like our community not withstanding all its struggles" (Letter to Paula Kilcoyne, March 20, 1990 [The Henri J. M. Nouwen Archives and Research Collection in the Special Collections and Archives, Toronto: John M. Kelly Library at the University of St. Michael's College, University of Toronto, Accession 2013 02]).

105 Sue Mosteller, letter to Henri Nouwen, May 7, 1990 (Letters Regarding The Return of the Prodigal Son, Henri Nouwen fonds, Manuscripts, Books, and Articles, the Henri J. M. Nouwen Archives and Research Collection, Box 23, File 1-59).

106 From "Notes from Meeting of May 8, 1990, re. Prodigal Son MS" in folder titled "Return of the Prodigal Son, Manuscript and Notes by Henri Nouwen" (unprocessed files in the Nouwen Archives).

107 Franz Johna, letter to Henri Nouwen, September 11, 1990 (the Henri J. M. Nouwen Archives and Research Collection, Accession 2012 55, Box 3), translation by Don Willms and Elisabeth Pozzi-Thanner; original German text: "*Der Aufbau is schön und harmonisch abgestimmt*."

108 Henri Nouwen, letter to William Barry, September 10, 1990 (Henri Nouwen fonds, Publisher Files, Doubleday Files, the Henri J. M. Nouwen Archives and Research Collection, Box 217, File 718). Nouwen writes in the same letter that he hopes Jackie Kennedy Onassis, then an editor at Doubleday, might visit Daybreak sometime in the near future. This didn't take place.

109 See p. 84.

110 Sue Mosteller, letter to Henri Nouwen, May 7, 1990, in response to first draft of *Prodigal Son* manuscript (Letters Regarding The Return of the Prodigal Son, Henri Nouwen fonds, Manuscripts, Books, and Articles, the Henri J. M. Nouwen Archives and Research Collection, Box 23, File 1-59).

111 From file "Drafts of The Return of the Prodigal Son [1991]" (Henri Nouwen fonds, Manuscripts, Books, and Articles, the Henri J. M. Nouwen Archives and Research Collection, Box 22, file 57-2). Language would become an issue, however. We will explore this more in an upcoming chapter.

112 Henri Nouwen, letter to Bill Barry ("Doubleday Correspondence File, 1990," Henri Nouwen fonds, Publisher Files, the Henri J. M. Nouwen Archives and Research Collection, Box 217, File 718).

113 Nouwen, letter to Bill Barry (File 719).

114 Nouwen, letter to Bill Barry (File 719).

115 Lannoo released the book with the title *Eindelijk Thuis: Gedachten bij Rembrandts "De terugkeer van de verloren zoon,"* which roughly translates as "Finally home: thoughts on Rembrandt's *Return of the Prodigal Son."* Herder released it as *Nimm Sein Bild in Dein Herz: Geistliche Deutung Eines Gemäldes von Rembrandt,* which translates as "Take his picture in your heart: spiritual meaning in the painting of Rembrandt."

116 Henri Nouwen, letter to Bill Barry, November 18, 1992 ("Doubleday Correspondence File, 1990," Henri Nouwen fonds, Publisher Files, the Henri J. M. Nouwen Archives and Research Collection, Box 217, File 720).

117 Fr. David Rothrock, Jean-Christophe Pascale, and Jean Vanier, "Report on the Mission to Daybreak to Evaluate the Place of Henri Nouwen as Priest of the Community" (December, 1991) (Henri Nouwen fonds, Calendar Files, Visit of Jean Vanier December 15–17, 1991, the Henri J. M. Nouwen Archives and Research Collection, Box 195, Files 1036), 2.

118 Carl Gustav Jung, "Archetypes and the Collective Unconscious," in *C. G. Jung: The Collected Works of C. G. Jung,* vol. 9, part 1, ed. Gerhard Adler and R.F.C. Hull (Princeton: Princeton University Press, 1980), 16.

119 Fox published two books on creation spirituality in 1991. In 1992, the year of the publication of *The Return of the Prodigal Son,* he published *Sheer Joy: Conversations with Thomas Aquinas on Creation Spirituality* (San Francisco: HarperSanFrancisco, 1992).

120 James Redfield, "My Story," James Redfield author page, https://www.celestinevision.com/2015/10/james-redfield/james-redfield-my-story/2/.

121 Marianne Williamson, *The Return to Love: Reflections on the Principles of a Course in Miracles* (New York: HarperCollins, 1992), 190. This quote is often attributed to Nelson Mandela's inaugural speech of 1994, but this is an erroneous attribution.

122 Williamson would acknowledge her overly bright conclusions in a new foreword to the book in 2017: "I'm older than I was when I wrote this book, and in some ways I am less innocent. I have tasted more of love's opposition. Yet having seen as much as I have now seen of the world's resistance to the ways of love, I realize more deeply than ever the responsibility which each of us has to embrace it more fully and express it effectively" (*Return to Love,* xii).

123 Edward Wyatt, "M. Scott Peck, Self-Help Author, Dies at 69," *New York Times*, September 28, 2005, https://www.nytimes.com/2005/09/28/books/m-scott-peck-selfhelp-author-dies-at-69.html.

124 M. Scott Peck, *The Road Less Traveled: A New Psychology of Love, Traditional Values, and Spiritual Growth* (New York: Simon and Schuster, 1978), 91–92.

125 It is worth noting that Siegel is the third author of this period to address miracles. Williamson's book, of course, is based on them, and Peck's *The Road Less Traveled* included many chapters on them as well.

126 It is striking how many male authors were born in or around January 1932, the year of Nouwen's birth.

127 Jung, "Archetypes and the Collective Unconscious," 16.

128 As quoted in Phyllis Theroux, "Use It or Lose It," review of *Care of the Soul* by Thomas Moore, *New York Times*, August 16, 1992, sec. 7, p. 25.

129 Theroux, "Use It or Lose It."

130 From Colleen O'Connor in the *Dallas Morning News*, extracted blurb for Thomas Moore, *Care of the Soul*, 25th-anniv. ed. (New York: HarperPerennial, 2016).

131 Moore has since written a foreword for a revised edition of Nouwen's book *Out of Solitude: Three Meditations on the Christian Life* (Notre Dame, IN: Ave Maria Press, 2004). He wrote, "Henri Nouwen has become a beloved spiritual writer for many people, and this book shows why. The power of his words takes a reader off to a place in imagination and emotion akin to a headland on the sea or a clearing in a forest or a low peak in a range of hills."

132 Clarissa Pinkola Estés, *Women Who Run with the Wolves: Myths and Stories of Wild Woman Archetype* (New York: Ballantine Books, 1995), 139.

133 In 1991, Patricia Hopkins and Sherry Ruth Anderson published *The Feminine Face of God* (New York: Bantam, 1991), which is about women's experiences of spirituality. In 1992, theologian Mary Daly (born four years before Henri Nouwen to a Catholic family) published *Outercourse: The Be-dazzling Voyage* (San Francisco: HarperSanFrancisco, 1992), which is part autobiography, part philosophy, and explores patriarchy in all its manifestations. Rosemary Radford Ruether would add a feminist take on this theme with *Gaia and God: An Ecofeminist Theology of Earth Healing* (San Francisco: HarperSanFrancisco, 1994), a few years after Fox published *Sheer Joy*. Fox, mentioned earlier, was an early pioneer in the field of eco-spirituality.

134 Nouwen famously went on the men's-group canoe trip in Algonquin Park (Ontario, Canada) with a suitcase on wheels. This story is wonderfully told by Carl MacMillan in "The Men's Group Camping Trip" in Porter, *Befriending Life*, 173–75.

135 Peterson is yet another author of interest who was born within a few months of Henri Nouwen. Peterson, in fact, was born within a month of Nouwen on November, 6, 1932. He died on October 22, 2018.

136 Just as Nouwen internalized visual imagery for spiritual sustenance and insight, Eugene Peterson encouraged people to memorize meaningful words. He had a practice of memorizing the Psalms. He also read and reread the works of Dickens and the poetry of George Herbert and Gerard Manley Hopkins.

137 David Richo, *How to Be an Adult: A Handbook on Psychological and Spiritual Integration* (Mahwah, NJ: Paulist Press, 1991), 3.

Chapter Four Notes 138–159

138 Henri Nouwen, letter to Bill Barry, November 18, 1992 (Henri Nouwen fonds, Publisher Files, Doubleday Files, the Henri J. M. Nouwen Archives and Research Collection, Box 217, File 720).

139 Henri Nouwen, letter to Ed Wojcicki, July 8, 1992 (Henri Nouwen fonds, General Files, the Henri J. M. Nouwen Archives and Research Collection, Box 144, File 8526).

140 Henri Nouwen, letter to Bill Barry, November 18, 1992 (Henri Nouwen fonds, Publisher Files, Doubleday Files, the Henri J. M. Nouwen Archives and Research Collection, Box 217, File 720).

141 Nouwen, letter to Bill Barry, November 18, 1992. L'Engle and Nouwen briefly exchanged letters shortly before Nouwen died. She had reached out to Nouwen suggesting they meet. Nouwen died before this could take place.

142 Bill Barry, letter to Lydia Banducci, July 20, 1993 (Henri Nouwen fonds, Publisher Files, Doubleday Files, the Henri J. M. Nouwen Archives and Research Collection, Box 217, File 720).

143 Luis R. Gamez, "The Return of the Prodigal Son: A Meditation on Fathers, Brothers, and Sons," *New Oxford Review* 59 (December 1992): 29.

144 See Michael Leach, "Hidden Treasure: The 10 Best Spiritual Books You've Never Read," *U.S. Catholic* 64, no. 4 (1999): 22–23. Other books on the list included *The Gift of Peace* by Joseph Cardinal Bernardin; *The Cloister Walk* by Kathleen Norris; *All Saints* by Robert Ellsberg; and *The Cup of Our Lives* by Joyce Rupp. Leach wrote, "All of Nouwen's many books will be read 10 years and 20 years and maybe even 50 years from now. Many of his faithful readers say this is one of his best" (23).

145 Names have been changed to protect privacy.

146 Embert Van Tilburg Sr., "Missing Son Is Victimized by Schizophrenia," *Prairie Messenger*, February 6, 1995, 16.

147 The complete letter was published in Henri Nouwen, *Love, Henri: Letters on the Spiritual Life*, ed. Gabrielle Earnshaw (New York: Convergent, 2016), 340–41.

148 O'Laughlin writes, "He was what Carl Jung and his followers call a puer aeternus, a person who remains childlike in adulthood" (Michael O'Laughlin, *God's Beloved: A Spiritual Biography of Henri Nouwen* [Maryknoll, NY: Orbis, 2004], 44). And, "Like the Little Prince or Peter Pan, Henri was a puer" (62).

149 From author's transcripts of "Returning" retreat, 10.

150 From a 2004 oral history interview with Claude Pomerleau, csc, by Errol Stein and Sue Mosteller.

151 Robert Moynihan in his book on Pope Francis, *Pray For Me: The Life and Spiritual Vision of Pope Francis, First Pope from the Americas* (New York: Image, 2013), mentions that the pope speaks highly of the works of Nouwen, specifically *The Return of the Prodigal Son* as cited in Zelda Caldwell, "Ten of Pope Francis' Favorite Books," *Aleteia*, March 1, 2018, https://aleteia.org/2018/03/01/10-of-pope-francis-favorite-books/2/.

152 Hillary Clinton, letter to Sue Mosteller, November 20, 1997 (Henri Nouwen Legacy Trust fonds, the Henri J. M. Nouwen Archives and Research Collection, Box 97), 67.

153 David Maraniss, "First Lady of Paradox," *Washington Post*, January 15, 1995, A26.

154 Hillary Rodham Clinton, "The First Lady on The Return of the Prodigal Son," *O, The Oprah Magazine*, July-August 2000, 217.

155 Hillary Rodham Clinton, *What Happened* (New York: Simon and Schuster, 2017). Other life-saving books included mysteries by Louise Penny, Jacqueline Winspear, Donna Leon, and Caroline and Charles Todd; novels by Elena Ferrante; and the collected poems of Maya Angelou, Marge Piercy, and T. S. Eliot.

156 Julia L. Roller, *25 Books Every Christian Should Read: A Guide to Essential Spiritual Classics* by Julia L. Roller (San Francisco: HarperOne, 2011). See p. 345 for the Rohr quote. Other books on the list: St. Athanasius, *On the Incarnation*; St. Augustine, *Confessions*; *The Sayings of the Desert Fathers*; *The Rule of St. Benedict*; Dante Alighieri, *The Divine Comedy*; plus C. S. Lewis, Thomas Merton, etc. Other lists have since been published, which include Nouwen's *The Return of the Prodigal Son* and *A Brief Guide to Spiritual Classics: From Dark Night of the Soul to the The Power of Now* (Robinson, 2016) by James M. Russell.

157 "Gulukkig niet een boek als *The Secret*," de *Verdieping Trouw*, November 23, 2011, https://www.trouw.nl/home/-gelukkig-niet-een -boek-als-the-secret-~aee0db14/.

158 Theo Lens, *Home at Last Project*, BOTB Records, 2015.

159 *A Volta do Filho Prodigo: O Musical* by Gerson Borges; *The Prodigal Son: A Rock Musical* by Paul Slagboom and Rene Steenkamp (2002); and Irma Dee, *Prodigal Daughter: A Story of Homecoming* (2017).

Chapter Five Notes 160–173

160 *Prodigal Son*, 126.

161 Mary Bastedo, "Henri and Daybreak: A Story of Mutual Transformation," in *Befriending Life: Encounters with Henri Nouwen*, ed. Beth Porter (New York: Doubleday, 2001), 31.

162 Bastedo, "Henri and Daybreak," 32.

163 Henri Nouwen, letter to Daybreak community, December 7, 1993 (Henri Nouwen fonds, Publisher Files, General Publisher Files, Miscellaneous Material 1993, the Henri J. M. Nouwen Archives and Research Collection, Box 227, File 848b).

164 Nouwen received upwards of thirty invitations a month. He formed a committee at Daybreak to help him discern which to accept and which to decline.

165 Nouwen, letter to Daybreak community, December 7, 1993.

166 Nouwen, letter to Daybreak community, December 7, 1993. Nouwen is referring to a sabbatical he was hoping to take between 1995 and 1996. It was approved. An account of this final year of his life is documented in the posthumously published *Sabbatical Journey: A Diary of His Final Year* (New York: Crossroad, 1998).

167 Some of these books were published posthumously.

168 The booklets are now published as *Finding My Way Home: Pathways to Life and the Spirit* (New York: Crossroad, 2001).

169 This is reminiscent of Nouwen's understanding of presence and absence in a pastoral setting or even death. He believed there is as much to be "given" in absence as in being present.

170 Wendy Lywood, "Rediscovering My Priesthood," in Porter, *Befriending Life*, 236.

171 Siobhan Keogh, "My Adopted Father," in Porter, *Befriending Life*, 158–59.

172 This section about Janet's blessing is from a story in Henri Nouwen's book *Life of the Beloved: Spiritual Living in a Secular World* (New York: Crossroad, 1992), 70–72. This version is based on a retelling by the Reverend Carlos Wilton on his website Wikipreacher. See Carlos

Wilton, "Nouwen Blesses All at L'Arche," Wikipreacher, http://www
.wikipreacher.org/home/quotations-and-illustrations/-b/blessing/
nouwen-blesses-all-at-l-arche. Sue Mosteller provided additional
details in conversation with the author, May 2019.

173 Henri Nouwen, letter to Bart Gavigan, December 2, 1994 (Henri
Nouwen fonds, General Files, the Henri J. M. Nouwen Archives and
Research Collection, Box 172, File 10670).

Chapter Six Notes 174–185

174 Italo Calvino, *The Uses of Literature* (San Diego: Harcourt Brace
Jovanovich, 1986), 128.

175 *Adam, Bread for the Journey, The Inner Voice of Love, Sabbatical
Journey, Can You Drink the Cup?*, and the notes for the Circus Book.

176 This is how E. H. Gombrich described Rembrandt in *The Story of Art*
(London: Phaidon, 1995), 420.

177 Conrad Wieczorek, memo to Henri Nouwen, May 12, 1990 (the Henri
J. M. Nouwen Archives and Research Collection, Accession 2012 55,
Box 3), 2.

178 Under no circumstances is Nouwen advocating for tolerance of abusive
behavior. Abuse—physical, or psychological—must be addressed with
decisive, protective action.

179 See *Prodigal Son*, 14.

180 Nouwen describes Rembrandt's God as a "very still Father" (*Prodigal
Son*, 89). God is "silent spaciousness" as understood by the poet David
Whyte.

181 It can also been seen as presaging the emergence of nonbinary people,
people who do not claim one gender or another. Nouwen alludes to
changes in people's attitudes toward gender difference in an AIDS talk
in 1994. See Carolyn Whitney-Brown's forthcoming book about Henri
Nouwen and the spirituality of the trapeze, *All of Life in Nine Minutes*,
97 (draft manuscript).

182 Henri Nouwen in interview with Michael Ford, BBC Radio 4, July
11, 1993 (Henri Nouwen fonds, Sound Recordings, the Henri J. M.
Nouwen Archives and Research Collection, SR128).

183 Nouwen writes, "The trapeze act was 'given' to me . . . . . . just as the
print of Rembrandt's 'The Return of the Prodigal Son' was 'given' to
me in 1983," in "Finding a New Way to Get a Glimpse of God: Circus
Diary, Part II," *New Oxford Review* 60, no. 6 (July-August 1993), 6.

184 Nouwen, "Finding a New Way to Get a Glimpse of God," 6.

185 What this book might have been is creatively imagined by Carolyn
Whitney-Brown in *All Of Life in Nine Minutes*, based on fragments of
the story Nouwen left behind.

Bibliography

This a listing of the published and unpublished works cited in the text of this book.

Secondary Sources

BOOKS

Bastedo, Mary. "Henri and Daybreak: A Story of Mutual Transformation." In *Befriending Life: Encounters with Henri Nouwen*, edited by Beth Porter with Susan M. S. Brown and Philip Coulter, 27–35. New York: Doubleday, 2001.

Berry, Carol. *Learning from Henri Nouwen and Vincent Van Gogh: A Portrait of the Compassionate Life*. Downers Grove, IL: InterVarsity Press, 2019.

Boers, Arthur. "L'Arche and the Heart of God." In *The Road to Peace: Writings on Peace and Justice by Henri Nouwen*, edited by John Dear, 151–59. Maryknoll, NY: Orbis, 1998. Originally published by *The Other Side* magazine as "Henri Nouwen: An Interview by Arthur Boers" in the special collection *Faces of Faith* (September-October 1989).

Calvino, Italo. *The Uses of Literature: Essays*. Translated by Patrick Creagh. San Diego: Harcourt Brace Jovanovich, 1986.

Clerx, Lily E., and Marinus H. Van Ijzendoorn. "Child Care in a Dutch Context: On the History, Current States and Evaluation of Nonmaternal Child Care in the Netherlands." In *Child Care in Context*, edited by Michael E. Lamb, Kathleen J. Sternberg, Carl-Philip Hwang, and Anders G. Broberg, 55–79. Hillsdale, NJ: Lawrence Eribaum, 1992.

Estés, Clarissa Pinkola. *Women Who Run with the Wolves: Myths and Stories of Wild Woman Archetype* (New York: Ballantine Books, 1995).

Gombrich, E. H. *The Story of Art.* 16th ed. New York: Phaidon, 1995.

Jung, Carl Gustav. "Archetypes and the Collective Unconscious." In *C. G. Jung: The Collected Works of C. G. Jung,* vol. 9, part 1, edited by Gerhard Adler and R. F. C. Hull, 3–41. Princeton: Princeton University Press, 1980.

Keogh, Siobhan. "My Adopted Father." In *Befriending Life: Encounters with Henri Nouwen,* edited by Beth Porter, with Susan M. S. Brown and Philip Coulter, 155–62. New York: Doubleday, 2001.

Lywood, Wendy. "Rediscovering My Priesthood." In *Befriending Life: Encounters with Henri Nouwen,* edited by Beth Porter, with Susan M. S. Brown and Philip Coulter, 232–37. New York: Doubleday, 2001.

Massie, Robert. "God's Restless Servant." In *Befriending Life: Encounters with Henri Nouwen,* edited by Beth Porter, with Susan M. S. Brown and Philip Coulter, 4–20. New York: Doubleday, 2001.

Nouwen, Henri. *Behold the Beauty of the Lord: Praying with Icons.* Notre Dame, IN: Ave Maria Press, 1987.

Nouwen, Henri. *Clowning in Rome: Reflections on Solitude, Celibacy, Prayer, and Contemplation.* New York: Doubleday, 1979.

Nouwen, Henri. *Home Tonight: Further Reflections on the Parable of the Prodigal Son: A Guide to Finding Your Spiritual Home.* Edited by Sue Mosteller, csj. New York: Doubleday, 2009.

Nouwen, Henri. *The Inner Voice of Love: Journey Through Anguish to Freedom.* New York: Doubleday, 1996.

Nouwen, Henri. *Intimacy: Pastoral Psychological Essays.* Notre Dame, IN: Fides, 1969.

Nouwen, Henri. *Life of the Beloved: Spiritual Living in a Secular World.* New York: Crossroad, 1992.

Nouwen, Henri. *Love, Henri: Letters on the Spiritual Life.* Edited by Gabrielle Earnshaw. New York: Convergent, 2016.

Nouwen, Henri. *Pray to Live: Thomas Merton; A Contemplative Critic.* Notre Dame, IN: Fides, 1972. Revised ed. published as *Encounters with Merton: Spiritual Reflections.* New York: Crossroad, 2005.

Nouwen, Henri. *The Return of the Prodigal Son: A Story of Fathers, Brothers and Sons.* New York: Random House, 1992.

Nouwen, Henri. *Sabbatical Journey: The Diary of His Final Year.* New York: Crossroad, 1998.

O'Donohue, John. *Anam Cara: A Book of Celtic Wisdom.* New York: HarperCollins, 1998.

O'Laughlin, Michael. *God's Beloved: A Spiritual Biography of Henri Nouwen.* Maryknoll, NY: Orbis, 2004.

Peck, M. Scott. *The Road Less Traveled: A New Psychology of Love, Traditional Values, and Spiritual Growth.* New York: Simon and Schuster, 1978.

Richo, David. *How to Be an Adult: A Handbook on Psychological and Spiritual Integration.* Mahwah, NJ: Paulist Press, 1991.

Roller, Julia L. *25 Books Every Christian Should Read: A Guide to Essential Spiritual Classics.* New York: HarperOne, 2011.

Williamson, Marianne. *The Return to Love: Reflections on the Principles of a Course in Miracles.* New York: HarperCollins, 1992.

ARTICLES

Asquith, Glenn H., Jr. "Anton T. Boisen and the Study of 'Living Human Documents.'" *Journal of Presbyterian History* 60, no. 3 (1980): 244–65.

Asquith, Glenn H., Jr. "Anton T. Boisen: A Vision for All Ages." College of Pastoral Supervision and Psychotherapy, January 25, 2016. A speech delivered at the CPSP Plenary, Chicago, Illinois, March 15, 2015. http://www.cpsp.org/pastoralreportarticles/3779024.

Asquith, Glenn H., Jr. "The Case Study Method of Anton T. Boisen." *Journal of Pastoral Care* 34, no. 2 (June 1980): 82–94.

Caldwell, Zelda. "10 of Pope Francis' Favorite Books." *Aleteia*, March 1, 2018. https://aleteia.org/2018/03/01/10-of-pope-francis-favorite -books/2/.

Clinton, Hillary. "The First Lady on The Return of the Prodigal Son." *Oprah Magazine*, July-August, 2000, 217.

Gamez, Luis R. "The Return of the Prodigal Son: A Meditation on Fathers, Brothers, and Sons by Henri J. M. Nouwen." Review of *The Return of the Prodigal Son* by Henri Nouwen. *New Oxford Review* 59 (December 1992): 28–29.

Gillespie, Kevin. "Psychology and American Catholicism After Vatican II: Currents, Cross-Currents and Confluences." *U.S. Historian* 25, no. 4, American Catholics and the Social Sciences (Fall 2007): 117–31.

"Gulukkig niet een boek als *The Secret*." *De Verdieping Trouw*, November 23, 2011. https://www.trouw.nl/home/-gelukkig -niet-een-boek-als-the-secret-~aee0db14/.

Leach, Michael. "Hidden Treasure: The 10 Best Spiritual Books You've Never Read." *U.S. Catholic* 64, no. 4 (1999): 22–23.

Leas, Robert D. "The Biography of Anton Theophilus Boisen." Association for Clinical Pastoral Education. https://www.acpe .edu/pdf/History/The%20Biography%20of%20Anton%20 Theophilus%20Boisen.pdf.

Leas, Robert D., and John R. Thomas. "A Brief History." Association for Clinical Pastoral Education. https://www.acpe.edu/pdf/ History/ACPE%20Brief%20History.pdf.

Maraniss, David. "First Lady of Paradox." *Washington Post*, January 15, 1995. https://www.washingtonpost.com/archive/politics/1995/01/15/ first-lady-of-paradox/dfc9f9e9-5905-4d16-8746-d3af4949c8b5/.

Nouwen, Henri. "Anton T. Boisen and Theology Through Living Human Documents." *Pastoral Psychology* 19, no. 186 (September 1968): 49–63.

Nouwen, Henri. "Finding a New Way to Get a Glimpse of God: Circus Diary, Part II." *New Oxford Review* 60, no. 6 (1993): 6–8, 10–13.

Nouwen, Henri. "Generation Without Fathers." *Commonweal*, June 12, 1970, 287–94. Reprinted in *Christian Education: Selections of Significance*. National Education Office, Canadian Catholic Conference, series 65, June 1, 1970, 7–8.

Pius XII. "On Psychotherapy and Religion." Encyclical Letter. 1953. Papal Encyclicals Online. http://www.papalencyclicals.net/pius12/p12psyre.htm.

Theroux, Phyllis. "Use It or Lose It." Review of *Care of the Soul*, by Thomas Moore. *New York Times*, August 16, 1992, sec. 7, p. 25.

Van Tilburg, Embert, Sr. "Missing Son Is Victimized by Schizophrenia." *Prairie Messenger*, February 6, 1995, 16.

Wyatt, Edward. "M. Scott Peck, Self-Help Author, Dies at 69." *New York Times*, September 28, 2005. https://www.nytimes.com/2005/09/28/books/m-scott-peck-selfhelp-author-dies-at-69.html.

SOCIAL MEDIA AND WEBSITE CONTENT

Freeman, Laurence. "Daily Wisdom—Aspects of Love 3." World Community for Christian Meditation, February 6, 2019. http://www.wccm.org/sites/default/files/users/Audio/2014B%20Aspects%20of%20Love%203%20-Master2.pdf?mc_cid=eaea6d5d86&mc_eid=b70be51029.

Redfield, James. "My Story." James Redfield author page. https://www.celestinevision.com/2015/10/james-redfield/james-redfield-my-story/.

Rohr, Richard. "Changing Perspectives—Jesus and the Cross." Center for Action and Contemplation, February 5, 2019. https://cac.org/changing-perspectives-2019-02-05/.

DISSERTATIONS

De Bono, Chris. "An Exploration and Adaptation of Anton T. Boisen's Notion of the Psychiatric Chaplain in Responding to Current Issues in Clinical Chaplaincy." PhD diss., University of St. Michael's College, 2012.

Primary Sources

MANUSCRIPTS

Nouwen, Henri. "Anton T. Boisen and Study of Theology Through Living Human Documents." Henri Nouwen fonds, Manuscripts, Books, and Articles, the Henri J. M. Nouwen Archives and Research Collection in the Special Collections and Archives. Toronto: John M. Kelly Library at the University of St. Michael's College, University of Toronto. Box 1, File 1-1-1-05.

Nouwen, Henri. "Boisen." In *Typescripts of Boisen Books*. Henri Nouwen fonds, Manuscript Series, the Henri J. M. Nouwen Archives and Research Collection in the Special Collections and Archives. Toronto: John M. Kelly Library at the University of St. Michael's College, University of Toronto. Box 1, File 01-2.

Nouwen, Henri. "Doubleday Correspondence File, 1990." Henri Nouwen fonds, Publisher Files, the Henri J. M. Nouwen Archives and Research Collection in the Special Collections and Archives. Toronto: John M. Kelly Library at the University of St. Michael's College, University of Toronto. Box 217, File 718, 719, 720.

Nouwen, Henri. *Draft of Circus Diary*. Henri Nouwen fonds, Manuscript Series, Books, and Articles, The Henri J. M. Nouwen Archives and Research Collection in the Special Collections and Archives. Toronto: John M. Kelly Library at the University of St. Michael's College, University of Toronto. Box 23, File 1-1-1-67.

Nouwen, Henri. "Drafts of The Return of the Prodigal Son [1991]." Henri Nouwen fonds, Manuscripts, Books, and Articles, the Henri

J. M. Nouwen Archives and Research Collection in the Special Collections and Archives. Toronto: John M. Kelly Library at the University of St. Michael's College, University of Toronto. Box 22, File 57-2.

Nouwen, Henri. *[First Draft of the Prodigal Son].* Henri Nouwen fonds, Accession files. Turner accession. The Henri J. M. Nouwen Archives and Research Collection in the Special Collections and Archives. Toronto: John M. Kelly Library at the University of St. Michael's College, University of Toronto. Accession 2010 63.

Nouwen, Henri. "Notes from Meeting of May 8, 1990, Re. Prodigal Son MS." Henri Nouwen fonds, Return of the Prodigal Son, Manuscript and Notes by Henri Nouwen. The Henri J. M. Nouwen Archives and Research Collection in the Special Collections and Archives. Toronto: John M. Kelly Library at the University of St. Michael's College, University of Toronto. Unprocessed file.

Nouwen, Henri. "Pastoral Supervision in Historical Perspective." Henri Nouwen fonds, Nouwen's Education Records and Study Documents, Menninger Clinic Records, the Henri J. M. Nouwen Archives and Research Collection in the Special Collections and Archives. Toronto: John M. Kelly Library at the University of St. Michael's College, University of Toronto. Box 287, File 1-8-4-306.

Rothrock, David, Jean-Christophe Pascal, and Jean Vanier. "Report on the Mission to Daybreak to Evaluate the Place of Henri Nouwen as Priest of the Community, December 1991." Henri Nouwen fonds, Calendar Files, Visit of Jean Vanier December 15–17, 1991, the Henri J. M. Nouwen Archives and Research Collection in the Special Collections and Archives. Toronto: John M. Kelly Library at the University of St. Michael's College, University of Toronto. Box 195, File 1036.

SOUND RECORDINGS

BBC Radio 4. "Recording of Henri Nouwen on Seeds of Faith: Henri Nouwen Talks with Michael Ford, July 11, 1993." Henri Nouwen fonds, Sound Recordings, Henri J. M. Nouwen Archives and Research Collection in the Special Collections and Archives. Toronto: John M. Kelly Library at the University of St. Michael's College, University of Toronto. Box 326, Item SR128. https://tspace.library.utoronto.ca/handle/1807/27424.

Nouwen, Henri. "Recording of Henri Nouwen on Returning: Reflections on the Prodigal Son." Henri Nouwen fonds, Sound Recordings, the Henri J. M. Nouwen Archives and Research Collection in the Special Collections and Archives. Toronto: John M. Kelly Library at the University of St. Michael's College, University of Toronto. Box 315, 322, Item SR84. https://tspace .library.utoronto.ca/handle/1807/27486.

ORAL HISTORY

Massie, Robert Kinloch. October 1, 2006. Interview by Sue Mosteller. Henri Nouwen Oral History Project fonds. The Henri J. M. Nouwen Archives and Research Collection in the Special Collections and Archives. Toronto: John M. Kelly Library at the University of St. Michael's College, University of Toronto. SR2007 68 42 30.

Pomerleau, Claude, CSC. Interview by Errol Stein and Sue Mosteller. October 22, 2004. Henri Nouwen Oral History Project fonds, the Henri J. M. Nouwen Archives and Research Collection in the Special Collections and Archives. Toronto: John M. Kelly Library at the University of St. Michael's College, University of Toronto. SR2007 67 73 60.

LETTERS

Barry, Bill G. Letter to Lydia Banducci, July 20, 1993. Henri Nouwen fonds, Publisher's Files, the Henri J. M. Nouwen Archives and Research Collection in the Special Collections and Archives. Toronto: John M. Kelly Library at the University of St. Michael's College, University of Toronto. Box 217, file 720.

Clinton, Hillary. Letter to Sue Mosteller, November 20, 1997. Henri Nouwen Legacy Trust fonds, the Henri J. M. Nouwen Archives and Research Collection in the Special Collections and Archives. Toronto: John M. Kelly Library at the University of St. Michael's College, University of Toronto. Box 97, File 67.

Egan, Joe. Letter to Henri Nouwen, December 4, 1985. Henri Nouwen fonds, the Henri J. M. Nouwen Archives and Research Collection in the Special Collections and Archives. Toronto: John M. Kelly Library at the University of St. Michael's College, University of Toronto. General Files, Box 87, File 4934. https://usmccollections.library.utoronto.ca/islandora/object/usmc2%3A1187.

Egan, Joe. Letter to Henri Nouwen, January 1, 1988. Henri Nouwen fonds, the Henri J. M. Nouwen Archives and Research Collection in the Special Collections and Archives. Toronto: John M. Kelly Library at the University of St. Michael's College, University of Toronto. Accession 2002 86, folder 12, 2.

Ellis, Connie. Letter to Gordon Turner, February 26, 1988. The Henri J. M. Nouwen Archives and Research Collection in the Special Collections and Archives. Toronto: John M. Kelly Library at the University of St. Michael's College, University of Toronto. Accession 2010 63.

Johna, Franz. Letter to Henri Nouwen, September 11, 1990. The Henri J. M. Nouwen Archives and Research Collection in the Special Collections and Archives. Toronto: John M. Kelly Library at the University of St. Michael's College, University of Toronto. Accession 2012 55, Box 3.

Mosteller, Sue. Letter to Henri Nouwen, February 28, 1988. The Henri J. M. Nouwen Archives and Research Collection in the Special Collections and Archives. Toronto: John M. Kelly Library at the University of St. Michael's College, University of Toronto. Accession 2002 86, folder 12.

Mosteller, Sue. Letter to Henri Nouwen and Nathan Ball, July 12, 1988. The Henri J. M. Nouwen Archives and Research Collection in the Special Collections and Archives. Toronto: John M. Kelly Library at the University of St. Michael's College, University of Toronto. Accession 2012 86, folder 12.

Mosteller, Sue. Letter to Henri Nouwen, May 7, 1990. Letters Regarding *The Return of the Prodigal Son*, Henri Nouwen fonds, Manuscripts, Books, and Articles, the Henri J. M. Nouwen Archives and Research Collection in the Special Collections and Archives. Toronto: John M. Kelly Library at the University of St. Michael's College, University of Toronto. Box 23, File 1-59.

Nouwen, Henri. Letter to Bart Gavigan, December 2, 1994. Henri Nouwen fonds, General Files, the Henri J. M. Nouwen Archives and Research Collection in the Special Collections and Archives. Toronto: John M. Kelly Library at the University of St. Michael's College, University of Toronto. Box 172, File 10670.

Nouwen, Henri. Letter to Bill Barry, November 18, 1992. Henri Nouwen fonds, Publisher Files, Doubleday Files, the Henri J. M. Nouwen Archives and Research Collection in the Special Collections and Archives. Toronto: John M. Kelly Library at the University of St. Michael's College, University of Toronto. Box 217, File 720.

Nouwen, Henri. Letter to Bill Barry, September 10, 1990. Henri Nouwen fonds, Publisher Files, Doubleday files, the Henri J. M. Nouwen Archives and Research Collection in the Special Collections and

Archives. Toronto: John M. Kelly Library at the University of St. Michael's College, University of Toronto. Box 217, File 718.

Nouwen, Henri. Letter to Carol Plantinga, November 26, 1985. Carol Plantinga fonds. The Henri J. M. Nouwen Archives and Research Collection in the Special Collections and Archives. Toronto: John M. Kelly Library at the University of St. Michael's College, University of Toronto. File 2010 23 01 03.

Nouwen, Henri. Letter to Daybreak Community, December 7, 1993. Henri Nouwen fonds, Publisher Files, General Publisher Files, Miscellaneous Material 1993, the Henri J. M. Nouwen Archives and Research Collection in the Special Collections and Archives. Toronto: John M. Kelly Library at the University of St. Michael's College, University of Toronto. Box 227, File 848b.

Nouwen, Henri. Letter to Daybreak Council, January 20, 1989. The Henri J. M. Nouwen Archives and Research Collection in the Special Collections and Archives. Toronto: John M. Kelly Library at the University of St. Michael's College, University of Toronto. Accession 2002 86, folder 12, 1-2.

Nouwen, Henri. Letter to Ed Wojcicki, July 8, 1992. Henri Nouwen fonds, General Files, the Henri J. M. Nouwen Archives and Research Collection in the Special Collections and Archives. Toronto: John M. Kelly Library at the University of St. Michael's College, University of Toronto. Box 144, File 8526.

Nouwen, Henri. Letter to Joe Egan. February 8, 1986. Henri Nouwen fonds, General Files, the Henri J. M. Nouwen Archives and Research Collection in the Special Collections and Archives. Toronto: John M. Kelly Library at the University of St. Michael's College, University of Toronto. Box 87, File 4934. https://usmccollections .library.utoronto.ca/islandora/object/usmc%3A67)

Nouwen, Henri. Letter to Paula Kilcoyne, March 20, 1990. The Henri J. M. Nouwen Archives and Research Collection in the Special

Collections and Archives. Toronto: John M. Kelly Library at the University of St. Michael's College, University of Toronto. Accession 2013 02.

Nouwen, Henri. Letter to Phillip Zaeder, July 7, 1989. Henri Nouwen fonds, General files, the Henri J. M. Nouwen Archives and Research Collection in the Special Collections and Archives. Toronto: John M. Kelly Library at the University of St. Michael's College, University of Toronto. Box 116, File 6605.

Nouwen, Henri. Letter to Richard, 1996. The Henri J. M. Nouwen Archives and Research Collection in the Special Collections and Archives. Toronto: John M. Kelly Library at the University of St. Michael's College, University of Toronto. Accession 2006 08.

Nouwen, Henri. Letter to Sue Mosteller, February 18, 1988. The Henri J. M. Nouwen Archives and Research Collection in the Special Collections and Archives. Toronto: John M. Kelly Library at the University of St. Michael's College, University of Toronto. Accession 2002 86, file 12.

Nouwen, Henri. Letter to Sue Mosteller, February 1988. The Henri J. M. Nouwen Archives and Research Collection in the Special Collections and Archives. Toronto: John M. Kelly Library at the University of St. Michael's College, University of Toronto. Accession 2002 86, file 12.

Nouwen, Henri. Letter to Sue Mosteller, March 4, 1988. The Henri J. M. Nouwen Archives and Research Collection in the Special Collections and Archives. Toronto: John M. Kelly Library at the University of St. Michael's College, University of Toronto. Accession 2002 86, file 12.

Wieczorek, Conrad. Memo to Henri, May 12, 1990. The Henri J. M. Nouwen Archives and Research Collection in the Special Collections and Archives. Toronto: John M. Kelly Library at the University of St. Michael's College, University of Toronto. Accession 2012 55, Box 2, 3.

Acknowledgments

Robert Ellsberg once quipped: "If ever there was a book that didn't need to be written it is this one," and readers familiar with *The Return of the Prodigal Son* will know the truth of this statement. Nouwen himself had already provided a compelling meta-narrative about how and why when he wrote the book. What more could be said? As it turns out, quite a lot. I am grateful to Jon Sweeney, editor of Paraclete Press, who saw the potential before I did. My thanks to Jon for his vision and for his skillful guidance of this project to completion. Thank you as well to the hard-working team at Paraclete Press including Michelle Rich, Rachel McKendree, and Jennifer Lynch.

Long before this book was written it was spoken. Taking a page out of Brené Brown's writing process, I gathered my friends Sue Mosteller, Lindsey Yeskoo, and Judith Leckie to be an audience of three while I groped my way to expression. Thanks to these three fine minds for their time, insights and humour. This book came into existence because of you—thank you! And yes, Judith, I still think *zeitgeist* is a great word, with no English equivalent!

I am also grateful to my beta readers Barbara Lloyd, Yannick Portebois, Karen Pascal, and Daphne Gray-Grant. This book was elevated by their careful reading and suggestions. Thank you as well to Liesl Joson and Simon Rogers at the Special Collections, Kelly Library for so ably facilitating my research in the Nouwen papers. Warren Pot and Siobhan Keogh helped with photograph identification. I extend my thanks.

As always, I was encouraged along the way by friends—thank you in particular to Robert Ellsberg and Carolyn Whitney-Brown for their words of advice and encouragement. They made all the difference.

Karen Pascal, Sally Keefe Cohen, and Judith Leckie of the Publishing Committee of the Henri Nouwen Legacy Trust must be acknowledged for their great support of this project; not only were they generous with permissions and access to archival documents, but also they encouraged me as friends at each stage of the process.

Finally, gratitude to my husband, Don Willms. Don is my first reader, but before that he is my listening ear, accompanying me each step along the long journey that is writing a book. He has heard more about Henri Nouwen than is fair but does so with humour and grace. Thank you, Don!

You may also be interested in...

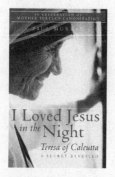

I Loved Jesus in the Night
Teresa of Calcutta A Secret Revealed
Paul Murray

ISBN 978-1-61261-895-1 | Trade paperback | $11.99

In his compelling account of meeting with the saint of Calcutta, Fr. Murray offers a glimpse into why Saint Teresa could declare that if ever she were to become a saint, she would surely be one of darkness.

Vulnerable and Free
An encouragement for those sharing in the life of Jesus
Fr. Paul Farren, Foreword by Timothy Shriver

ISBN 978-1-64060-200-7 | Trade paperback | $12.99

"My heart was caught off guard by this wise and heart opening reflection on the transformative, if often unwelcome, power of powerlessness."
—Timothy Shriver

More Stories of Great Books...

Victorious
Corrie ten Boom and *The Hiding Place*
Stan Guthrie

ISBN 978-1-64060-175-8 | Trade paperback | $16.99

This is the story of how Corrie ten Boom's 1971 classic, *The Hiding Place*, came into being, sold millions, and helped shape the faith of a generation.

Available at bookstores
Paraclete Press | 1-800-451-5006 | www.paracletepress.com